Barbecue!

From the Reynolds Wrap Kitchens

Random House New York

Pictured left to right: Susan C. Gaible, Carol Owen and Ann Tretiak

Friends,

In today's busy lifestyle, we have found that almost everyone wants to know how to barbecue with ease — but few have the time to uncover the "secrets" and learn the "family tested techniques." The Reynolds Wrap Kitchens have spent hundreds of hours testing techniques and methods. We have compiled only the best for you in this book.

You don't need years of experience; we've taken most of the guesswork out of the cooking methods. You can use the extra minutes to relax and enjoy your meal. Whether you're cooking a low-budget dinner or a clambake, you'll find many step-by-step instructions to help you.

There are many variables for you to consider when cooking your meals in the great outdoors, whether its your own backyard or at a national campground. For best results, consider the time of year, temperature of the coals, the type of grill, cut of meat and whether the grill is lined with aluminum foil. All of these factors influence your finished product. For meats, we find the meat thermometer is the most accurate measure for doneness. Your trusty eye will give you vegetables and other foods cooked to perfection.

From our kitchens to yours,

Susan C. Gaible

Susan C. Gaible
Manager, Consumer Services, **The Reynolds Wrap Kitchens**

Copyright © 1983 by Consumer Division, Reynolds Metals Company
All rights reserved under International and Pan-American Copyright Conventions.
Published in the United States By Random House, Inc., New York and simultaneously in Canada by Random House of Canada Limited, Toronto.

Originally published by Reynolds Metals Company in 1982

Library of Congress Cataloging in Publication Data

" Originally published by Reynolds Metals Company in 1982'' --T.p. verso.
   Includes Index.
   1. Barbecue Cookery. I. Title: Reynolds Wrap Kitchens.
TX840.B3B34   1983   641.5'784   82-48960   ISBN 0-394-53137-X

Manufactured in the United States of America
         24689753   First Edition

Contents

Barbecue Basics 7

Grills 8

Accessories 14

The Fire 21

Grilling Techniques 24

Time Saving Ideas 30

Marinades, Sauces & Butters 32

Beef 36

Pork 42

Ribs 48

Sausages 50

Lamb 52

Poultry 54

Fish & Seafood 62

Kabobs 72

Game 76

Vegetables 80

Breads & Desserts 86

Appetizers & Snacks 92

Planning Your Event 94

Complete Grill Meals 96

Index 110

Barbecue!

from the Reynolds Wrap Kitchens

Barbecue Basics

Begin with the basics and barbecuing is easy. Once you know the simple rules of cooking out-of-doors, you're ready for anything over the coals.

Basics start with choosing the right type of equipment for the foods you plan to grill. Today there are at least five basic types of grills, each with a wide variety of special features and options that increase the grill's versatility. Select the type that fits your lifestyle best. Learn to use all of the features on your grill like air vents, adjustable grids and fire pans, and covers to increase your grilling finesse.

Besides the grill, there are accessories and utensils designed to handle even the most delicate foods and make outdoor cooking a cinch. Start with tongs, fork and spatula, then work your way up to the more unusual racks and baskets. Always keep a box of Heavy Duty Reynolds Wrap® aluminum foil and a supply of Redi-Pan® foilware for convenient wrapping and disposable containers.

No matter what you plan to cook or what type of grill you own, one of the most important basics is knowing how to build and light the fire. Once you have an evenly burning bed of coals, charcoal cooking the complete meal is simple. Remember to wait for coals that are ashy grey by day or glowing red by night before cooking, then begin your favorite foods by using the proper techniques.

Anytime of year is barbecue time. There's nothing more cheerful than a mid-winter fireplace cook-in with friends and family. And now, covered grills make barbecuing out-of-doors a year-round activity.

Glossary of Terms

Ash Catcher: A pan used to catch ashes from grill. May be inside or outside grill base.

Cover: Found on square cookers and kettles. Helps retain heat inside grill, control flare-ups.

Direct Cooking: Method of grilling foods directly over coals. Heat may be high, medium or low. Best for quick-cooking foods like burgers, chops, steaks, page 21.

Drip Pan: A pan used to catch juices and prevent flare-ups. It can be a Redi-Pan or molded from a sheet of Heavy Duty Reynolds Wrap.

Ember Cooking: Method of cooking vegetables directly in glowing coals, page 28.

Fire Pan: Holds the coals. Usually a separate container under grid, but in basic grills like hibachis and braziers, the grill itself can be the fire pan.

Grid: Stainless steel rack over coals that holds food that is to be cooked.

Hood: Wind screen commonly found on braziers. Meant for protecting fire and food from wind. Some have notches for rotisserie. Hood can be made from Heavy Duty Reynolds Wrap, page 18.

Indirect Cooking: Method of grilling by arranging coals around or to one side of drip pan. Drip pan is placed directly under food, page 21.

Spit or Rotisserie: Accessory for rotating food over fire. Can be battery or electrically powered.

Vents: Holes in top of hood and bottom of grill with stainless steel or aluminum covers for regulating air flow and temperature of coals.

Grills

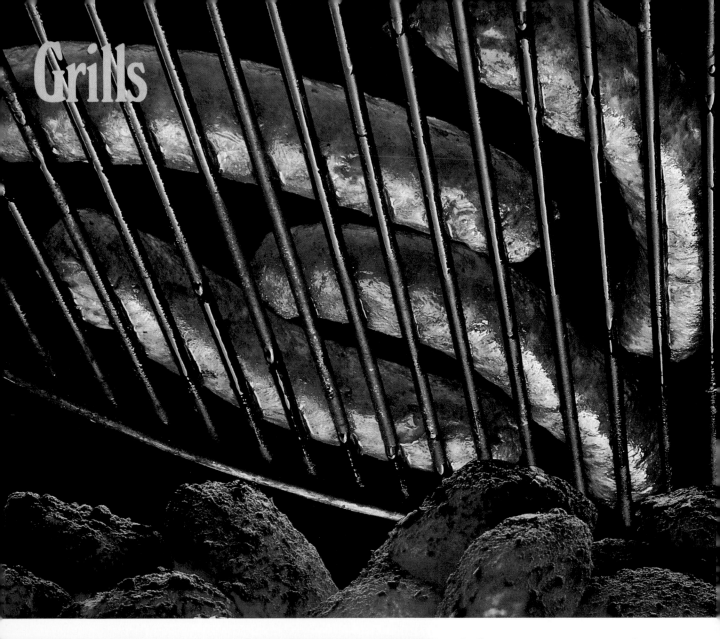

Grills come in a variety of shapes and sizes. The grill you pick depends on your style of living and entertaining. The chart at right lists some things to consider before you buy. Refer to your use and care manual for proper usage.

1. Gas Grill
2. Hooded Brazier
3. Square-Covered Cooker
4. Water Smoker
5. Portable Picnic Grill
6. Kettle Cooker

8

Selecting a Grill

Size	If cooking for two is more your style, then a small portable kettle or hibachi will do. If you enjoy big parties, choose a large grill with some of the "frills."
Food	Choose an open brazier if you cook small cuts of meat, such as steaks and chops. Choose a square-covered cooker or kettle for cooking larger cuts of meat, such as roasts and turkey.
Storage	Think about where you will store your grill ... backyard barbecue center ... or balcony?
Finish	For durability and easy care, seek out porcelain enamel finish. Less expensive, less durable is painted steel which needs to be stored out of the weather and wiped clean after each use to prevent staining and corrosion.
Weather	If you're a year-round griller (and why not?) look for a durable covered grill. These retain heat better and make cook-out eat-in parties possible even in winter.

The Open Brazier

Any uncovered grill falls into this category but the larger hooded brazier pictured is popular. Some braziers boast half-hoods, covers, electric or battery-operated rotisseries.

Small tabletop hibachis can also be considered open braziers. When feeding a large crowd, an extra brazier is handy. The heat is regulated by adjusting grid to regulate distance of food from coals. Line the grill with Heavy Duty Reynolds Wrap® for even heat distribution and fast cleanup.

Three Ways to Use Your Brazier

1. Direct Cooking. Line grill with Heavy Duty Reynolds Wrap. Position hot coals directly under food and cook quickly.

2. Rotisserie. Arrange coals around outer edge of fire pan with heavy duty foilware drip pan or Redi-Pan® on grid adjusted to lowest position. Remove drip pan when cool.

3. Spit basket. Use flat spit basket to cook smaller foods like salmon steaks, pork steaks, delicate whole fish. Oil rack lightly to prevent sticking.

The Covered Cooker

Round, square or rectangular, the covered cooker is wonderfully versatile. Without the cover, it does everything a brazier does. With the cover, it will roast, steam, smoke and cook whole meals. The cover reduces turning, watching, fussing and flare-ups. It retains heat, so you can use the cooker in any kind of weather.

Look for an adjustable fire pan or grid and vented cover for heat control. The wooden handles make lifting the cover easier and safer.

Three Ways to Use Your Covered Cooker

1. Uncovered. Remove cover and your kettle cooker or square-covered cooker will double as a brazier for searing and quick-cooking.

2. Covered. Add cover to slow-cook larger cuts and whole meals. Adjust heat by raising or lowering fire pan or grid, or opening or closing vents.

3. Rotisserie. Adjust lid to half open for square cookers with rotisserie. Cover can be completely closed also, but be sure vents are open.

The Water Smoker

A heavy dome-type grill with water pan, the smoker is among the newest types of grills to become widely available. They are popular among sportsmen for cooking game and fish. Foods are kept moist and juicy while they're slowly cooked with charcoal briquets and hickory chips or your favorite aromatic wood.

The water smoker operates with the use of two pans, a water pan and a charcoal pan. The water pan is placed about 12 inches over the coals. When grill is covered, steam rises in a "cloud" to permeate food. Food cooks for hours, basking in the aromatic vapor from the coals.

Some water smokers have additional stack units to cook several layers of food simultaneously. Gas and electric water smokers are also available.

Two Ways to Use Your Water Smoker

1. Brazier. The water smoker grill also doubles as an open brazier for quick cooking. Remove water pan and place fire pan with coals directly under the food.

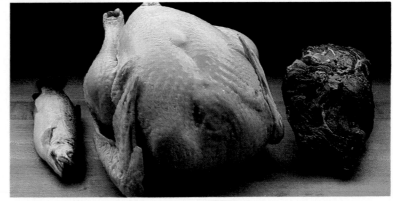

2. Water smoker. Smoke fish, game and larger meat cuts in a water smoker for extra hickory-smoked flavor. It offers a no-watch kind of cooking which results in incomparable flavor and moistness.

Portable, Tabletop Grills

Many people start barbecuing with a relatively inexpensive portable grill, then progress to a more elaborate one. The simplest grills, these are small grid-topped models which can be supported on folding or collapsible legs. They're light, easy to clean and store, and come in 12-, 14- and 18-inch sizes.

Great strides have been made in recent years to perfect the portable grill. Choices now run the gamut. Pictured: 1. Tabletop covered kettle, 2. Boat grill, 3. Stand-up hibachi, 4. Fireplace grill, 5. Portable open brazier and 6. Hibachi.

The Gas Grill

The greatest advantage of a gas grill is the convenience. The fire is ready at once, no wait for the "coals" to reach proper cooking temperature. Generally, the initial investment is higher than a charcoal grill. Gas grills now come in smaller portable tabletop models as well as larger backyard models.

Lava rock or ceramic briquets are heated by the gas flame, and cook just like charcoal.

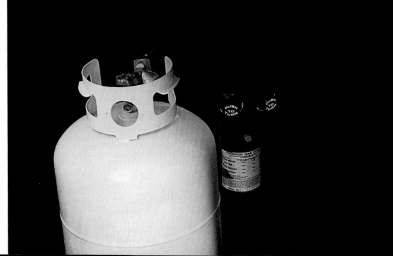

Accessories

The right barbecue accessories are not extras, they're essential. Having the right tool for the right task is safer, as well as more convenient. Barbecue accessories are made from stainless steel wire that is designed to be easy to clean and easy to handle. The right accessories allow you to barbecue food you never expected to cook on the grill. Keep your barbecue accessories in a special place. Hang a utensil rack on your grill so tools are handy.

14

1. Meat thermometer
2. Long-handled basting brush
3. Heavy duty cooking mitt

4. Seasonings
5. Water spritzer
6. Long-handled tongs

7. Aluminum foil saucepan
8. Roasting rack

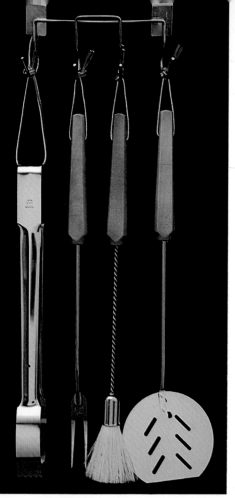

Begin With the Basics

No matter what you plan to grill, certain accessories are as necessary as the grill and the charcoal. They add up to a safer, easier and more exciting cookout. And when it comes time to clean up, the right tools can hasten the chore.

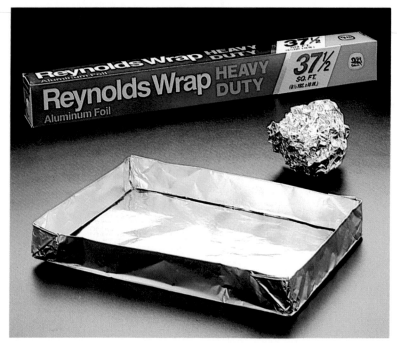

Utensils should have wooden or thermoplastic handles. Good starter set: two sets of tongs (for coals, food), long-handled fork, spatula, basting brush and utensil holder for hanging.

Heavy Duty Reynolds Wrap is one indispensable tool. Use it to line the grill before adding briquets. The aluminum foil protects the grill and promotes even cooking. It also serves as a wrap for ashes. Use a crumpled piece of foil to clean messy grids by rubbing foil along rack. A foil drip pan catches meat juices, prevents flare-ups. It can also be used to bake biscuits, stir-fry or sauté vegetables.

Charcoal starters are available in electric, liquid and chimney-type. The chimney needs only newspaper. Electric is convenient and fast.

Hot pads and cooking mitts should be heavy duty and handy. Extra long mitts are ideal for handling hot grills and protecting hands from splatters.

Baking soda and a water spritzer are ideal for extinguishing flare-ups. Spray water directly at coals or sprinkle baking soda over coals after removing food.

16

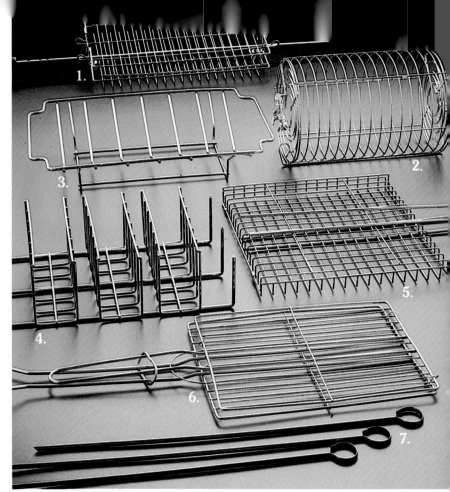

Disposable aluminum foil-ware comes in several shapes and sizes. Use it for catching meat juices, cooking cut-up vegetables, warming baked beans and fruit desserts. Ideal for serving directly from the grill.

Wire accessories add convenience. The Flat Spit Basket, 1, and Tumble Basket, 2, are powered by rotisserie and are ideal for delicate fish. A roast Rack, 3, promotes even cooking, lets you lift out roast easily. Rib Racks, 4, increase cooking area by as much as 50%. Hinged Grill Baskets, 5 and 6, with long handles hold fragile foods securely and make turning easier. Long-handled skewers, 7, are ideal for kabobs.

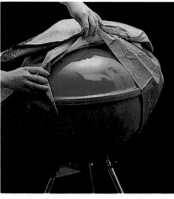

Meat thermometers are available in two styles, quick register and meat probe. They are used to insure rare, medium and well cooked meats on the grill.

Rotisseries increase versatility of grill. The slow turn is excellent for browning and basting roasts and whole birds.

Vinyl covers protect your grill from bad weather. Available in sizes to fit most types of grills. They are an inexpensive way to add years to the life of your grill.

17

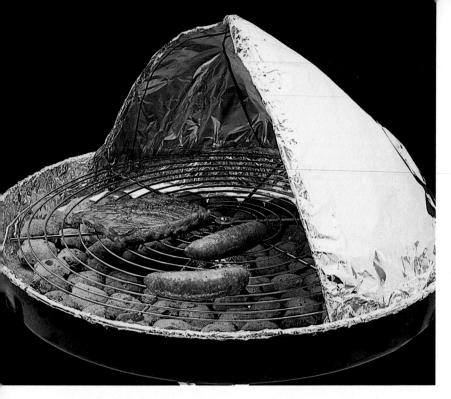

Accessories You Can Make

Occasionally, even the best-equipped kitchen finds itself without the necessary utensil. That's the time to reach for Heavy Duty Reynolds Wrap.® Not only can aluminum foil be used as a covering or wrap for foods, but since it is so sturdy, it can also be used for making wind screens, hoods, cooking containers and utensils.

Aluminum foil reflects heat, providing an even heat distribution.

How to Make an Aluminum Foil Hood

Clip off hooks of six or seven coat hangers; straighten. Form a circle using two or more. It should fit just inside the grill.

Loop remaining wire, umbrella fashion, and attach to the circle. Use pliers to twist the ends. Fasten together at top with wire.

Cover wire umbrella frame with Heavy Duty Reynolds Wrap, leaving a small portion loose at top to open and close for temperature control.

How to Make an Aluminum Foil Wind Shield

Follow above directions for making wire umbrella frame. Pull back wire loops on one side of frame to form a half circle. Secure loops in place with wire.

Cover the half frame with Heavy Duty Reynolds Wrap. Place the windguard inside the edge of the grill to block wind and help maintain a steady fire.

Remove aluminum foil when soiled; re-cover frame with clean aluminum foil for reuse.

Saucepot. Mold three layers of heavy duty aluminum foil around bowl to form desired size. Remove bowl and fold edges down to form tight rim. Use to warm beans, soup, extra sauce. Remove from grill using pot holders in both hands.

Drip Pan or Baking Pan. Tear off two sheets of heavy duty aluminum foil. Double fold edges forming 1½- to 2-inch sides. Score and miter corners for strength. Use as drip pan in coals or as baking pan on grid.

Reynolds Wrap Hamburger Press. Tear off a sheet of heavy duty aluminum foil 12 inches long. Fold in a series of 1-inch folds to make a 1×12-inch strip. Crimp and fold ends together forming a 3-inch ring. Gently pat in ground beef.

The Fire

Follow the pyramid method for lighting standard briquets. For instant lighting briquets follow package directions. *An evenly burning bed of coals is the secret to maintaining control over your cookouts.* Many foods require different cooking temperatures, so learn to judge temperature of the coals before you place food on the grill. Always grill in a well ventilated area.

Once the coals have reached the correct cooking temperature, they can be spread for cooking in either the direct or indirect methods. When cooking foods that require longer cooking times, use tongs to add 10 to 12 briquets to edges of burning coals every hour to maintain heat. Different brands of briquets give off varying degrees of heat, so cooking times will always be approximate. Follow techniques on page 23 for controlling the temperature.

Line the grill with Heavy Duty Reynolds Wrap® for even heat distribution and easy cleanup. First lay a sheet long enough to cover grill from side to side then crisscross with another sheet of aluminum foil. Fold over edge of grill and crimp. Cut out openings to conform with grill vents.

How to Arrange a Direct and Indirect Fire (cutaway view)

Direct cooking. Arrange coals directly under food, extending 1 inch beyond edge of food for direct method.

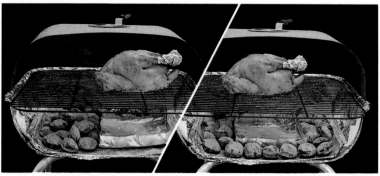

Indirect cooking. For slow indirect cooking in covered grill, or on rotisserie, place coals to one side of the grill with an aluminum foil drip pan placed under food, pictured above left. For hotter indirect cooking place drip pan in center of coals, pictured above right.

How to Determine the Number of Coals to Use

Determine the number of coals needed by spreading single layer of coals 1 inch beyond edge of food for small cuts of meat. Heap more charcoal for longer cooking foods.

Stack coals in a pyramid to light the fire. Pyramid shape provides enough ventilation for coals to catch. Be sure all coals are touching each other.

Ignite briquets with a starter made for charcoal briquets. Choose from liquid, wax/jelly, chimney or electric starters. Let coals burn until ashy grey before cooking.

Latest in barbecue aids, instant lighting briquets start faster, need no charcoal starter.

Three Common Types of Starters

Liquid. Sprinkle liquid starter on briquets, allow to soak in for about 45 seconds; light with match. Pre-soaking briquets in a coffee can aids lighting, too.

Wax or jelly. Squeeze over and under briquets. Light briquets before starter evaporates. Shake can before using to loosen wax.

Electric. Nestle into coals. Watch while briquets begin to turn grey. Always remove starter from coals after 8 minutes to avoid burn-outs.

How to Use a Chimney Starter

Place crumpled newspaper in bottom of chimney starter. Leave several newspaper ends sticking out of holes in chimney base. Fill top of chimney with charcoal briquets.

Light newspaper ends with a match. Flames will spread up through chimney to light briquets. Let burn without disturbing for 10 to 15 minutes.

Remove starter when all briquets have begun to turn ashy grey or are glowing by night. Use insulated hot pads when picking up chimney. Spread coals in single layer with tongs.

How to Know if Coals are Ready

Ashy grey coals by day mean fire is hot and it's time to begin cooking. For most even cooking, never grill while some coals are still black.

Glowing red by night also says it's time to cook. As temperature falls at night, keep coals closer together to maintain heat. Tap ash off as coals burn down to maintain heat.

Thermometer on top of dome lid of smoker grill indicates the internal temperature. Keep an eye on it throughout cooking.

Judge Fire Temperature

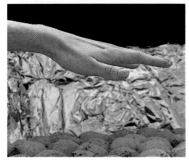

Judge temperature by cautiously holding your hand, palm side down, over coals at grid level. Count the seconds that you can hold the position.

Fire Temperature Chart

Seconds Hand Held Over Fire	Fire Temperature is
5 seconds	Low
4 seconds	Medium
3 seconds	Medium-High
2 seconds	Hot

How to Adjust Heat

Control Air Flow. Vent holes in a covered grill control air flow throughout. To raise the temperature, open vents fully. To lower the temperature, close halfway. To snuff out coals, close vents entirely.

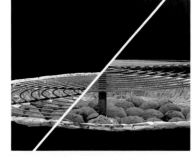

Control Grid Height. Distance of food from coals will affect cooking temperatures. Lower the grid for more intense heat and quick cooking. Raise the grid for longer, slower cooking without charring.

Control Closeness of Coals. In addition to distance, closeness of coals to each other affects temperature. To lower temperature, spread coals further apart. To increase heat, bank closer together and tap ash.

Temperatures to Begin Cooking

Heat	Temp. of Coals	Grid Height	Foods
Low	Med.-Low	High	**Beef:** Roasts; **Desserts; Seafood:** Clams, Oysters, skewered
Medium	Med.-Low	Medium	**Beef:** Cubes; **Lamb:** Cubes, Leg; **Lobster; Pork:** Chops, Cubes, Roasts; **Poultry:** Pieces, Whole birds; **Pre-Baked Fruit Pies; Sausages:** Bologna, Hot dogs (Franks), Pork links (pre-cooked); **Vegetables**
High	High	Low	**Beef:** Burgers; **Pork:** Ribs; **Toasting:** Rolls

Note: To retain juiciness, thick cuts of meat should be seared on high, then cooked at medium or low heat to finish.

Grilling Techniques

Open Brazier Method

This cutaway grill illustrates the simplest method of barbecuing. The open brazier relies on direct heat. It is excellent for foods requiring quick searing like steaks, burgers, chops, hot dogs. Think of it as broiling outdoors. *Wait until coals die down to the ashy grey stage before placing food on grid.*

Since many open braziers come without grids for controlling temperature, learn to use the hand hold test for judging temperature of coals. Smaller braziers like hibachis and picnic grills require fewer coals so don't overload. And in case of fat flare-ups, have a water pistol handy. With open brazier cooking, foods should be no more than 5 inches from the coals.

24

Covered Cooking

This method, also called dry smoking, is similar to roasting in an oven, only with charcoal as the source of heat. Food is cooked by heat reflected from the cover, as well as with heat from the coals. Food is surrounded by a uniform, controlled heat that substantially cuts cooking time and allows meat to maintain its natural juiciness and flavor. The covered cooker is excellent for whole birds, roasts, whole fish and vegetables.

As a technique, covered cooking is one of the most versatile methods. It may be done in a square, rectangular or kettle cooker. The indirect method is often applied to covered cooking. Plan whole meals from main dish to dessert for the covered cooker.

25

Rotisserie Cooking

Plug-in or battery-powered rotisserie gives old-fashioned done-to-a-turn flavor to meat, fish and poultry. For most even cooking, be sure meat is balanced and secure on spit. Readjust if needed. Surest grip may involve placing prongs at one end at right angles to prongs at other end. Place aluminum foil drip pan to front of grill to catch meat juices. For detailed rotissing instructions on poultry, see page 59; for pork, page 49; for beef, page 41.

Rotisserie Techniques

Spit basket. Use spit basket for slowly cooking delicate fish and vegetables. Lightly oil basket before adding food to avoid sticking. Brush food with butter or margarine for moistness.

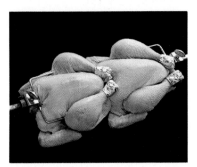

Small birds. Mount two small birds rather than one large bird on spit for easier handling and quicker cooking times. Butt birds together legs to shoulders for compactness and balance.

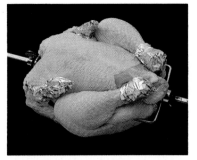

Foil shielding. Avoid charred wings or legs. Secure them with string before spitting birds. Wrap aluminum foil around wing tips and leg ends to prevent burning.

Basting. Apply marinades and sauces with a long-handled brush. Baste frequently.

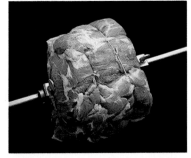

Balancing. Look for evenly shaped cuts of meat to ensure even roasting. See page 59 for balance test.

Drip pan. Keep fat out of the fire and catch drippings with a drip pan shaped from a double thickness of Heavy Duty Reynolds Wrap,® page 19.

Smoke Cooking

Smoke cooking refers to grilling done in a water smoker-type grill. A water pan placed between food and coals creates a "cloud" around food which permeates meats and vegetables for added smoky flavor. Layering meats and vegetables lets you cook complete meals. Intensify the flavor with a few drops of liquid smoke added to the water pan or sprayed on meat and coals. Since water smoking can take as long as 10 hours, add fresh coals to fire every hour to maintain heat. Remove lid as seldom as possible, each peek adds about 15 minutes to cooking time. Follow manufacturer's directions for cooking times.

To ease cleanup, line charcoal pan with Heavy Duty Reynolds Wrap® before lighting the fire.

Add dampened hickory chips to hot coals before cooking food in a water smoker. They add flavor and help create steam that will rise to food. Pour natural liquid hickory smoke into water pan for added flavor.

Smoked Turkey and barbecued baked beans in molded saucepot.

Ember Cooking

Cooking vegetables directly in the coals gives them a wonderful woodsy flavor.

Always oil skins lightly before cooking. For some thinner-skinned types, Drugstore Wrap in Heavy Duty Reynolds Wrap.® Cooking times vary according to temperature of coals. To reduce charring of vegetable skins, wrap in aluminum foil and cook over low temperature using minimum number of coals to surround vegetables. Prick with fork to test doneness.

How to Ember Cook Vegetables

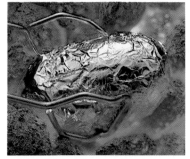

Potatoes. Rub scrubbed, dry potato skins with oil or margarine. Drugstore Wrap in heavy duty aluminum foil. Cook 45 to 55 minutes until soft when pricked. Turn occasionally.

Squash. Nestle whole butternut or acorn squash in hot coals. Turn occasionally. Roast 45 to 60 minutes. Open, remove seeds; butter. Season with nutmeg, mustard or brown sugar.

Corn. Remove silk; soak corn-in-husks in ice water for 30 minutes. Shake off excess water. Roast corn with or without aluminum foil directly in coals 35 to 45 minutes; turn often.

How to Ember Cook an Onion

Trim off ends of medium to large size onion. Remove any loose skins.

Bury in coals; cook until black and soft to fork pressure, about 1¼ hours. Use tongs to remove onion to cool surface.

Slip off charred skin and discard. Onion inside will be smoky-delicious! Eat while hot.

Wrapping Techniques

Choosing the right fold for foil-barbecuing food calls for common sense. Foods which create a lot of steam or expansion (like popcorn) should have a loose Bundle Wrap. Foods which require frequent turning will fare better in Drugstore Wrap. Either way, Heavy Duty Reynolds Wrap® aluminum foil is a versatile tool for cooking and serving.

Wrap foods with either shiny or dull side of aluminum foil out. Difference in appearance does not affect performance.

How to Bundle Wrap

Center odd shapes and some types of moist food on a square of heavy duty aluminum foil that's roughly three times the size of the food.

Bring four corners up together into a pyramid shape. Fold opening together loosely. Be sure to allow room for heat circulation and expansion.

Seal by folding over ends and pressing to package. Keep upright to avoid leakage. Wrap is especially good for irregular-shaped foods.

How to Drugstore Wrap

Place food in center of oblong piece of heavy duty aluminum foil large enough to allow for folding at top and sides.

Bring two sides together above food; fold down in a series of locked folds, allowing for heat circulation and expansion.

Fold short ends up and over again and crimp close to package to seal. This reduces leakage and cooks food evenly.

Time Saving Ideas

Save cooking time with combination cooking. While coals burn to cooking stage, micro-cook larger cuts of poultry and meat. Then complete cooking on grill. Sear before adding sauce.

Cook several meals when you use the smoke cooker by layering foods. Extras can be microwaved later in the week.

Sear an extra steak or chicken over charcoal for flavor and color. Wrap in Heavy Duty Reynolds Wrap® and freeze. To serve, unwrap and microwave until sizzling. Brush with flavored butter.

Cover grills to speed up cooking. Aluminum foil hoods and covers can be improvised for coverless grills, page 18.

Start the fire safely in 20 minutes or less by using a chimney-type starter, page 22.

Self-lighting briquets save steps, time and eliminate the need for a charcoal starter.

Choose small cuts of meat or small birds for meals in a hurry. Larger cuts need a covered grill and longer cooking time.

Charcoal-cook extra servings of meat for quick, no fuss lunch next day. Slice, chop or grind for delectable sandwiches.

Combine prepared barbecue sauces or marinades with herbs. They are the secret to preparation in a hurry.

Marinate less tender beef steaks using packaged or bottled marinade mixes.

Bake refrigerator biscuits in a covered grill. Use an aluminum foil baking pan placed over medium-low, indirect heat; cover grill.

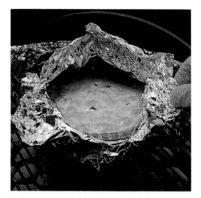

Warm up a baked fruit pie in an aluminum foilware pie pan. Bundle Wrap with aluminum foil to protect flavors. Place over medium coals in a covered grill.

Grill a pizza. Bake on a Redi-Pan® Pizza Pan in a covered grill over medium coals.

Bundle Wrap your favorite combination of meats and vegetables to form a complete meal cooked on the grill.

Use recyclable Redi-Pan aluminum foilware. Available in many shapes and sizes, they are sturdy and practical.

Line a small table with Heavy Duty Reynolds Wrap.® Use as a grill-side work table.

31

Marinades, Sauces & Butters

Enhance foods with marinades, sauces and butters. Marinades stretch budgets by tenderizing and flavoring inexpensive cuts of meat. Marinades work by penetrating meat fibers and should always contain an acid or alcohol base such as vinegar, fruit juice, wine or beer.

Look for flavor balance in a marinade. Marinades can be cooked or uncooked. Cooked marinades should be chilled before adding to meat. Pour in enough marinade to immerse meat halfway, then cover dish.

How to Marinate

Marinate in refrigerator overnight, but no longer than 24 hours. Turn occasionally. Cubed meats should be marinated only 2 to 3 hours. Cover.

Brush both sides of the meat with extra marinade during cooking. Use an aluminum foil saucepot, page 19, to keep the marinade warm.

Marinade Chart

Use ½ cup of marinade for each pound of meat.

Type	Method: combine the following ingredients	Use On
Apple Tarragon 2 cups	1 cup apple cider, ⅓ cup vinegar, ⅓ cup sliced green onions with tops, ¼ cup vegetable oil, 3 tablespoons honey, 2 tablespoons steak sauce, 1½ teaspoons tarragon leaves, 1 teaspoon salt and ¼ teaspoon freshly ground pepper. Bring to a boil, simmer uncovered 20 minutes. Chill before using.	Chicken Lamb
Beer 2 cups	1 can (12 oz.) beer, ½ cup vegetable oil, 2 tablespoons cider vinegar, 1 small onion, thinly sliced, 2 cloves garlic, minced, 1 teaspoon salt and ½ teaspoon freshly ground pepper.	Beef
Curry Apple 1 cup	1 cup applesauce, 2 tablespoons lemon juice, 2 teaspoons curry powder, 1 teaspoon salt and ¼ teaspoon pepper.	Lamb
Mint Honey 1 cup	⅔ cup dry white wine, ⅓ cup honey, 1 tablespoon vinegar, 1 clove garlic, minced, 1½ teaspoons chopped fresh mint and 1 teaspoon salt.	Lamb
Onion Soup 1 cup	1 envelope onion soup mix, ½ cup vegetable oil, ¼ cup cider vinegar, 1 teaspoon sugar and 1 teaspoon Worcestershire sauce.	Beef
Pineapple 1½ cups	1 can (6 oz.) or ¾ cup unsweetened pineapple juice, ½ cup dry sherry, 2 tablespoons brown sugar, 1 clove garlic, minced and ½ teaspoon rosemary leaves.	Pork
Red Wine 2 cups	1 cup red wine, ⅔ cup vegetable oil, ½ cup finely chopped onion, 2 cloves garlic, minced, 1 teaspoon salt and ½ teaspoon freshly ground pepper.	Beef
Teriyaki 1½ cups	½ cup soy sauce, ⅓ cup dry sherry, ⅓ cup firmly packed brown sugar, ¼ cup vinegar, 2 tablespoons vegetable oil, 1 clove garlic, minced and ½ teaspoon ground ginger.	Beef Chicken Pork Seafood
White Wine 2 cups	¾ cup dry white wine, ¼ cup lemon juice, ¾ teaspoon salt, ½ teaspoon pepper and ½ teaspoon dry mustard.	Fish

Herb Butter on barbecued chicken, page 35

Sauces

Sauces are used to flavor foods. They are brushed on during cooking, and unlike marinades, have no tenderizing qualities. Sauces come in a range of flavors, from sweet to savory.

A good sauce is very rich in flavor to sharpen outdoor appetites. When making a sauce from scratch, use first-class ingredients, not tired leftovers.

Sugar-based glazes and sauces will burn quickly and should be brushed on during the last 15 minutes of grilling. Keep sauces within easy reach of food that you are preparing.

Pork Chops basted with Hot and Spicy Sauce, below.

Sauce Chart

Type	Method	Use On
Apple Curry 1⅔ cups	In a saucepan, combine 1 jar (10 oz.) apple jelly, ⅓ cup dry white wine, ¼ cup sliced green onions with tops, 2 tablespoons prepared mustard, ½ teaspoon salt, ½ teaspoon curry powder and ½ teaspoon freshly ground pepper. Heat until jelly has melted, stirring occasionally.	Chicken Lamb
Apricot Ginger 1½ cups	Combine 1 jar (12 oz.) apricot preserves, 3 tablespoons cider vinegar, 2 tablespoons melted butter, ½ teaspoon ground ginger and ½ teaspoon salt.	Chicken Pork
Cucumber 1¼ cups	Combine ¾ cup peeled, diced cucumber, ¼ cup dairy sour cream, ¼ cup mayonnaise, 1 tablespoon sliced green onion, 1 teaspoon grated lemon peel and ¼ teaspoon dill weed. Cover and refrigerate to blend flavors.	Chicken Fish Pork
Hot and Spicy 2 cups	In a saucepan, combine 1 can (8 oz.) tomato sauce, ⅓ cup vinegar, ⅓ cup packed brown sugar, 2 tablespoons prepared mustard, ½ cup chopped onion, 1 clove garlic, finely chopped and 1 tablespoon chili powder. Bring to boil; simmer 5 minutes.	Chicken Hamburger Pork Steak
Pineapple 1⅓ cups	In a saucepan, combine 1 can (8¼ oz.) crushed pineapple and 2 teaspoons cornstarch; stir. Add 3 tablespoons honey, 2 tablespoons soy sauce and 2 tablespoons cider vinegar. Heat 5 minutes.	Chicken Pork
Tangy Beer ⅔ cup	Combine ⅓ cup chili sauce, ¼ cup beer, 2 teaspoons prepared horseradish, ½ teaspoon sugar, ½ teaspoon salt, ¼ teaspoon pepper, ½ teaspoon instant minced onion and ¼ teaspoon dry mustard.	Hamburger Steak

Butters

Plan an assortment of butters so guests can choose their own. Serve butter two ways: melted and brushed on hot, or room temperature and spread with knife. Always soften butter to room temperature before adding flavorings or use margarine. Tub-type margarines are ready at once. Add butter to second side of meat during last stages of cooking to prevent burning.

Butter Chart

Type	Method: Combine the following ingredients	Use On
Blue Cheese	¼ cup softened butter, ½ cup crumbled blue cheese, 1 clove garlic, minced, 1 tablespoon sliced green onions.	Hamburgers Steak
Cheese Herb	½ cup softened butter, 3 tablespoons Parmesan cheese, 1 tablespoon finely chopped parsley, ½ teaspoon basil leaves, ¼ teaspoon garlic powder.	Corn-on-the-cob Sliced zucchini Vegetable bundles
Cinnamon Sugar	¼ cup softened butter, ¼ cup firmly packed brown sugar, ½ teaspoon cinnamon, ¼ teaspoon nutmeg, ½ teaspoon grated lemon peel, 1 teaspoon lemon juice.	Bread Sliced apple or banana bundles
Garlic	½ cup softened butter, 1 tablespoon finely chopped parsley, 1 teaspoon garlic powder.	Shrimp Sliced bread Steak
Herb	½ cup softened butter, 2 tablespoons sliced green onions, 2 tablespoons chopped parsley, ½ teaspoon tarragon leaves, ¼ teaspoon salt.	Chicken Fish Mushrooms Vegetable bundles
Mustard	½ cup softened butter, ¼ cup Dijon mustard, 1 tablespoon sliced green onions with tops, ¼ teaspoon garlic powder, ¼ teaspoon pepper, dash Worcestershire sauce.	Beef Duck
Parsley Orange	½ cup softened butter, 1 tablespoon grated orange peel, 1 tablespoon orange juice, 1 tablespoon honey, 2 teaspoons chopped parsley.	Chicken Duck Lamb

How to Use Butters

Spread Cheese Herb Butter, above, on corn and other vegetables inside aluminum foil bundles before cooking. Steam circulates the flavors.

Brush Herb Butter, above, on fish before wrapping in foil packet to keep from drying out. Use a brush with a long wooden or thermoplastic handle.

After cooking lightly score surface of steak. Spread with seasoned butter for more flavor.

Beef

Barbecuing beef is one of the best ways to bring out its hearty, rich flavor. Charcoal grilled beef should be crispy on the outside and juicy on the inside. Sear quickly over hot coals to lock in juices. Finish over medium to medium-hot coals.

Barbecuing the Perfect Burger

For regular size burgers, use open brazier; do meat-loaf size "burgers" in a covered cooker.

For juicy burgers, choose higher fat cuts, chuck or sirloin. Round (about 15% fat) is lower-calorie. Try some wonderful combinations: onion, avocado, cheese condiments, soy sauce, horseradish, you name it. To prevent meat from sticking to grid, oil rack lightly.

Be creative with your favorite hamburger variation; chart below

Hamburger Variations

Mix With Beef	Stuff Your Burger*	On Top of Burger	Bun
Taco sauce	Monterey Jack cheese with jalapeño peppers	Sour cream, avocado slices, cooked bacon	Sesame bun, butter
Chopped onions, salt, pepper	American cheese	Heated, canned chili	Kaiser roll, butter
Salt, pepper	Capers, cooked bacon	Spinach leaves	English muffin
Catsup, mustard, salt, pepper	Sliced kosher pickles	Swiss cheese	Onion bagel, mustard
Salt, pepper	Chopped onion	Chopped lettuce and tomato, Thousand Island dressing, cucumbers	Dark rye or pumpernickel bread
Worcestershire sauce, salt, pepper	Blue cheese	Chopped tomato, sliced onion, cucumber, leaf lettuce	Kaiser roll, Dijon mustard
Chopped mushrooms, basil leaves	Mozzarella cheese	Pizza sauce, chopped olives	Italian bread, butter

*Note: Stuff by placing ingredients between two ½-inch uncooked patties. Seal edges and grill as directed. Stuffers may be used as toppers if unstuffed hamburgers are preferred.

How to Barbecue Burgers

Pack ground beef lightly into aluminum foil press. Overhandling causes tough burgers. See page 19. Make ½-inch (2 oz.) to 1-inch (4 oz.) thick patties.

Arrange burgers 4 to 6 inches from hot coals. Spritz flare-ups with water mister.

Sear ½-inch thick burgers 2 minutes on first side; 1-inch thick burgers 3 minutes. Turn only once and cook until done.

Rare burgers need 4 minutes of searing on second side over medium coals.

Medium burgers need 6 more minutes on second side if ½ inch thick, 7 more minutes if 1 inch thick.

Well done burgers may need 12 more minutes on open brazier after searing. Cut slit in center to judge doneness.

Brush sauce on burger while grilling, then again after turning, if desired.

When burgers are done with a beef timer, chef's hat pops up.

Place buttered buns, cut side down, around edges of grill to toast. Guests can add their own toppings as desired.

Steak

Who can resist a hot, sizzling barbecued steak! A steak for barbecuing should be at least 1 to 2 inches thick. For a crowd, do one large steak or individual steaks to taste. Try marinating less expensive steaks such as chuck, round and flank for great flavor. For extra special flavor, top a steak with seasoned butters.

How to Barbecue Steaks

Trim excess fat. Slash remaining fat just to (not into) meat. Place on grill about 4 inches from hot coals to sear.

Turn the steak using long-handled tongs. (Do not use a fork or juices will escape.)

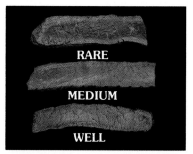

Check doneness with a beef timer, page 39, or by slitting close to bone. Carve thin slanting slices for tenderness.

Steak Chart

Cut and Thickness	First Side	Second Side
Club, Rib, Rib-eye, T-bone, Porterhouse, Sirloin 1¼-inch	Sear on high, direct heat. 3 to 5 minutes.	Medium to low heat.* Rare: 8 minutes Medium: 10 minutes Well: 12 to 15 minutes
Top round, Chuck 1¼-inch	Marinate and/or tenderize. Sear on high, direct heat. 5 to 8 minutes.	Medium to low heat.* Rare: 7 to 10 minutes Medium: 12 minutes Well: 15 minutes
Flank steak ½-inch	Score both sides; marinate. Sear on high, direct heat. 5 minutes.	High direct heat. 5 minutes.
London broil (1st cut top round) 2-inch	Marinate and/or tenderize. Sear on high, direct heat. 8 minutes.	Medium to low heat.* Rare: 20 minutes Medium: 22 minutes

*To lower temperature, increase distance from fire and cover grill, if desired.

Beef Roasts

Use indirect method or rotisserie over a constant medium to low heat to barbecue beef roasts. Shield bony tips with aluminum foil to prevent burning. Check doneness with a meat thermometer. For easier carving, remove the roast from the grill and let it rest on a carving board about 15 minutes before slicing.

How to Barbecue Roasts

Choose a well-marbled, evenly contoured roast. Trim so fat is no more than ½ inch thick. Cook either on rotisserie or in covered cooker.

Rotisserie. Tie roast into uniform shape. Push spit lengthwise through meat; fasten with holding forks. Place aluminum foil drip pan in coals beneath and in front of roast.

Covered Cooker. Place roast into rack and place on grid. Use aluminum foil drip pan and grill by the indirect method. Add cover or aluminum foil hood and grill until done.

Beef Roast Chart

Use medium to low, indirect heat.

Cut and Weight	Time	Internal Temp.
Beef rib roast 4 to 6 lbs.	Rare: 14 to 16 min./lb. Medium: 16 to 20 min./lb.	140°F. 160°F.
Boneless beef roast: **Round rump,** **Round tip,** **Chuck cross-rib pot roast** 4 to 6 lbs.*	Rare: 20 to 22 min./lb. Medium: 23 to 25 min./lb.	140°F. 160°F.
Fresh beef brisket, **Flat half, boneless**** 4 to 7 lbs.	4½ to 6 hours	140°F.

*Marinate roast 4 hours or overnight in refrigerator.
**Use charcoal water smoker. Follow manufacturer's instructions.

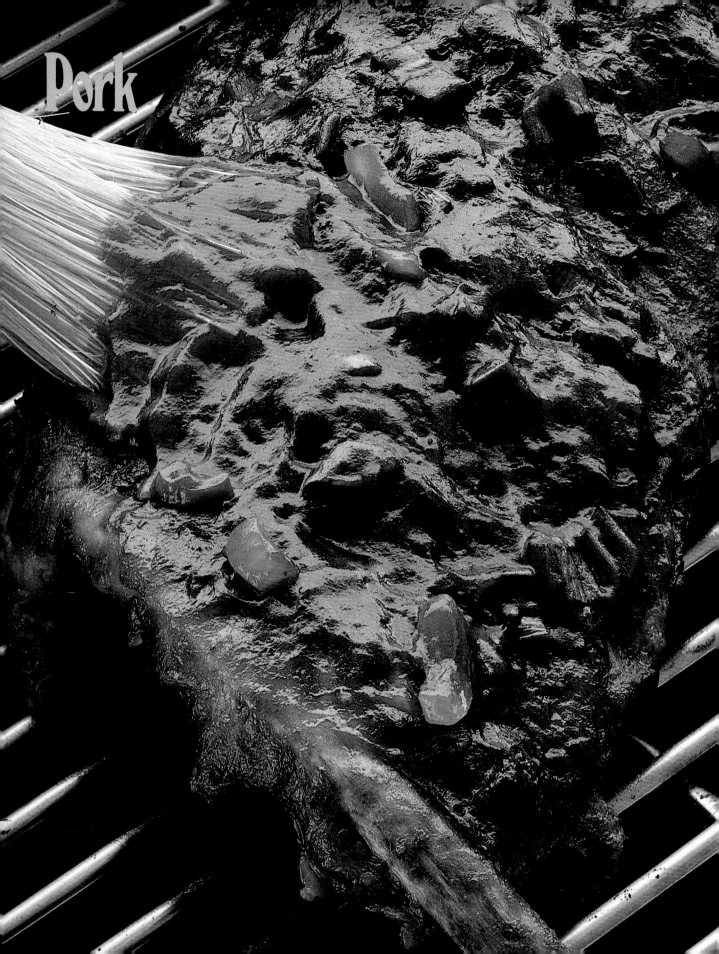

Pork

The slow roast of a covered kettle or water smoker is ideal for barbecuing pork. The best pork is grilled slowly over low to medium coals. Pork is often a more economical choice for feeding crowds, so don't overlook smoky pork chops, whole pork roasts, seasoned pork burgers, racks or rotisserie spits full of ribs when planning an outdoor menu.

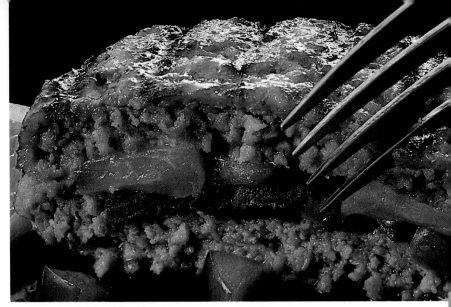

Polynesian-Stuffed Pork Burger; chart below

How to Prepare Ground Pork for Barbecuing

Combine ¼ pound ground beef to every pound ground pork for juiciest burgers. Pick seasoning from chart below.

Season ground pork with liquid smoke, onion, garlic, sage, pepper, lemon, shredded cheese, mustard or your idea.

Stuff filling between two ½-inch thick uncooked patties. Seal edges and grill as directed.

Pork Burger Chart

Use medium, direct heat.

Type Burger	Season Pork with	Stuff Center with	Baste with
American	Liquid smoke, chopped onion, salt, pepper	American cheese	Combined catsup and prepared mustard
Chinese	Chopped fresh parsley, garlic powder, sage, salt, pepper	Sliced water chestnuts	Teriyaki sauce
Italian	Parmesan cheese, pepper	Sliced mushrooms	Pizza sauce
Mexican	Chopped green chilies, salt, pepper	Monterey Jack cheese	Taco sauce
Polynesian	Soy sauce, salt, pepper	Pineapple ring, chopped green pepper	Pineapple juice

Note: Buy lean ground pork or ask your butcher to grind pork from a Boston pork shoulder roast.

Personalize bottled sauce by adding chopped onions and spices.

Teriyaki Marinade on pork chops, page 33

How to Prepare Pork Chops

Slash the fat on pork chops just to the meat. This prevents curling. Trim off any excess fat.

Stuff a 2-inch thick pork chop with a savory stuffing. Cut a pocket from rib side to center of chop, cutting parallel to surface.

Marinate pork not so much for tenderness as for deep-down flavor. Brush on marinade during cooking, also.

General Tips on Grilling Pork

Pork manufacturers are processing leaner meat. To insure best results grill slowly 4 to 6 inches from medium to low coals. Cook until juices run clear.

Pork Chops, Steaks and Burgers Chart

Cut and Size	Time	Method
Ground Pork Burgers ½ inch thick	15 to 20 minutes	**For all cuts:** make a bed of medium to low coals. (High, searing heat will toughen pork and smoked ham.) Grill first side about half recommended time over direct heat or until browned. Turn and season or baste with sauce, if desired. Grill until done, but still juicy and tender. (Do not overcook or pork will be dry and tough.)
Pork Kabobs 1¼ inch cubes	15 to 20 minutes	
Rib, Loin Chops ¾ to 1 inch thick	20 to 30 minutes	
Shoulder Blade Steaks ¾ to 1 inch thick	25 to 35 minutes	
Smoked Loin Chops 1 inch thick	15 to 20 minutes	
Ham Steaks 1 inch thick	25 to 30 minutes	**Foil-Wrapped:** Drugstore Wrap ham slice. If desired, top with canned apricots, fresh apple slices, brown sugar and butter.

Pork Roasts

Pork roasts, boneless or bone-in, taste delicious when barbe-cued. They cook slowly and evenly in covered grills, water smokers, or on rotisseries. For easy carving, buy a boned, rolled loin. Cook all pork roasts over low to medium heat to an internal temperature of 170°F for juicy, tender pork. Let rest for 15 minutes before carving.

46

Two Methods for Grilling Pork Roasts

1. Rotisserie. Buy a roast that's a good size and shape to skewer. Boned roasts work best. Be sure prongs hold roast securely.

2. Roasting. Indirect heat in a covered cooker is another alternative for barbecuing roasts. A light basting is desirable.

Roasting on the Covered Grill

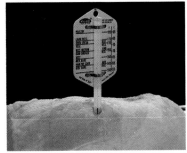

Flavor roast by tossing damp hickory chips, garlic cloves or onion skins onto coals. With cover down flavor permeates meat.

Use a meat thermometer to tell doneness of roasts. Insert thermometer into thickest part of meat not touching bone or fat.

Use a roast rack when barbecuing a roast in a covered grill. It allows for even cooking and simplified lifting.

Pork Roast Chart

Use medium to low, indirect heat.

Type/Size Roast	Time	Internal Temp.	Method
Bone-in: Pork loin, Pork butt, Pork shoulder 3 to 5 lbs.	15 to 18 min./lb.	170°F	Use rotisserie or cover grill.
Boneless: Pork loin, Pork butt, Pork shoulder 3 to 5 lbs.	22 to 25 min./lb.	170°F	Use rotisserie or cover grill.
Fully Cooked Ham 3 to 5 lbs.	15 to 18 min./lb.	140°F	Cover grill.
Smoked Ham Half Cook-before-eating 5 to 7 lbs.	22 to 25 min./lb.	160°F	Remove rind and score fat diagonally before cooking. Stud with cloves if desired. Cover grill.
Rib Crown Roast unstuffed 7 to 8 lbs.	13 to 16 min./lb.	170°F	Place in baking pan directly on grid. Cover grill. Use direct, medium to low heat.

Ribs

The most famous "down home" barbecue recipe is likely to be one for ribs. Succulent and crusty, ribs make finger-lickin' eating. The three main kinds of ribs are spareribs, country-style ribs and back ribs. Spareribs are often a bit more expensive per pound. Fortunately, the same sauces work equally well with all sorts of ribs. Find your favorite — and enjoy!

Ribs with Hot and Spicy Sauce, page 34

How to Steam Ribs

Steam ribs before grilling to render out fat. Place ribs in double thickness of Heavy Duty Reynolds Wrap® with 2 tablespoons water. Drugstore Wrap. Seal tightly.

Place aluminum foil packet with ribs over the hot coals. Grill for ¾ to 1 hour in either a covered cooker or on an open brazier. Do not open the packet during steaming.

Lift packet from grill to table. Drain fat. Remove ribs from aluminum foil packet. Finish either on open brazier or in covered grill, below.

Open Brazier Method and Covered Cooker Method

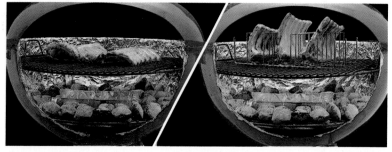

Open Brazier. Place drained ribs directly on grid. Brush during cooking with sauce or marinade. Apply sweet sauces during last 15 minutes to avoid burning.

Covered Grill. Grill drained ribs either indirectly on grid over drip pan, pictured above left, or place in rib rack, pictured above right. Baste occasionally during cooking with long-handled brush. Cook with cover down.

Three Ways to Grill Ribs

1. Spareribs. Cook a rack of spareribs on the rotisserie by threading it accordion-style on the spit.

2. Country-Style Ribs. Grill country-style ribs upright in a rib rack. Close grill cover for best results.

3. Baby Back Ribs. Cut slab into servings of four ribs each. Place in rotisserie basket and let them tumble as they cook.

Rib Chart

Allow 1 to 2 servings per pound of ribs.

Type	Time	Method
Baby Back Ribs (cut in serving-size sections)	Foil Bake: ¾ hour Grill: ½ to 1 hour	Foil-bake over high, direct heat. Remove from aluminum foil. Coat well with barbecue sauce. Place in rotisserie basket. Use medium-low, indirect heat. Baste several times with barbecue sauce.
Country-Style Ribs (cut in serving-size sections)	Foil Bake: 1 hour Grill: ½ to 1 hour	Foil-bake over high, direct heat. Remove from aluminum foil. Season with salt, pepper, and garlic powder. Place on grid. Cover grill. Use medium-low, indirect heat. Baste with barbecue sauce.
Spareribs	Foil Bake: ¾ hour Grill: ½ to 1 hour	Foil-bake over high, direct heat. Remove from aluminum foil. Place on grid or in rib rack. Use medium-low, indirect heat. Baste with barbecue sauce.
Beef Ribs	Use same method as Country-Style Ribs, above.	

Sausages

Mixed Grill

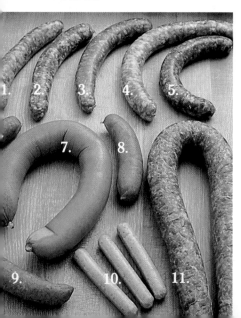

There are as many different types of sausages as there are nationalities. The kind and amount of processing that a sausage receives determines its storage and cooking requirements. Always check the label or with the butcher to see if sausage is cooked or uncooked.

As a rule, fresh sausage requires precooking to remove some of the natural fat. Precooked fresh sausage can then be grilled over a drip pan and medium, indirect heat. Fully cooked sausage may be grilled over medium, direct heat without a drip pan or precooking.

Sausage Types for Grilling:

Fresh sausage: 1. bratwurst, 2. Polish sausage, 3. Italian pork sausage, 4. country-style pork sausage, and 5. Spanish chorizos.

Fully cooked sausage: 6. franks, 7. bologna, 8. knockwurst, 9. cooked bratwurst, 10. brown-and-serve sausage links and 11. Polish kielbasa

50

How to Barbecue Sausages

Precook fresh sausages with 1 or 2 tablespoons of water. Drugstore Wrap. Steam over medium coals 10 minutes, pictured above left. Finish cooking over an aluminum foil drip pan to catch drippings and prevent flare-ups, pictured above right. For best results, turn often, until evenly browned on all sides.

Split large fully cooked sausages in half lengthwise, cutting down but not all the way through. Grill over medium, direct heat 10 to 15 minutes, turning frequently.

Grill fully cooked sausages directly over medium coals, turning frequently. Cook until browned and heated through.

Serve a mixed grill for lunch. Precook fresh sausages over fire first; add fully cooked sausages during last 15 minutes. Nice menu additions are hot German potato salad, cooked in aluminum foil on the grill, or chilled, seasoned sauerkraut.

Smoke franks in a water smoker. Prick skins and arrange on grill. Cook 2 to 3 hours or until internal temperature of 160°F, turning occasionally.

Breakfast on brown-and-serve sausage links and eggs. Brown sausage quickly over direct heat. Place aluminum foil baking pan on grid and add butter. Place sausage in pan, break in the eggs, and cook until firm. Season. On cool day, cover with aluminum foil.

Lamb

Barbecued lamb is distinctive when you want an extra special cookout. It has just the right amount of marbling to let grilling proceed smoothly, and the flavor of lamb is enhanced by charcoaling. Lamb can be transformed with seasonings and marinades of various kinds or grilled "as is" with a sprig of fresh mint.

Try chops and steaks, cubes for kabobs, butterflied leg of lamb and ground lamb for an unforgettable cookout.

Apple Tarragon Marinade on lamb chop, page 33

How to Cook Different Cuts of Lamb

Chops/Steak. Marinate 4 hours or overnight for extra flavor. Grill chops over medium, direct heat.

Cubes. Marinate lean lamb cubes from the leg or shoulder and skewer with vegetables. Grill over medium, direct heat.

Roasts. Barbecue large cuts like boneless leg, shoulder and loin in covered grill or rotisserie. Use medium, indirect heat; baste often.

52

Lamb Chart

Cut	Time	Method
Boneless loin, Shoulder roasts 4 to 5 lbs.	Rare (140°F): 20 min./lb. Medium (160°F): 22 min./lb. Well Done (170°F): 25 min./lb.	Grill in covered cooker or rotisserie over medium coals. Place aluminum foil drip pan under meat to catch drippings for gravy. Brush frequently with favorite sauce.
Chops, Steaks ¾ to 1 inch thick	13 to 16 minutes	Place on grid. Use medium, direct heat.
Kabobs from leg 1¼-inch cubes	13 to 16 minutes	Marinate 4 hours or overnight in refrigerator. Thread cubes on skewers. Place on grid. Use medium, direct heat. Baste with favorite sauce, see page 33 and 34.
Leg of lamb, boned, rolled and tied 4 to 5 lbs.	Same times as Shoulder roasts, above.	Marinate lamb. Place on grid. Cover grill. Use medium, indirect heat. Turn and baste occasionally with marinade.

Lamb Sauces and Seasonings Chart

Type	Method
Barbecue Sauce	Combine ⅓ cup catsup, ¼ cup chili sauce, 1 tablespoon finely chopped onion, 1 tablespoon finely chopped green pepper, 1 tablespoon brown sugar, and 1 tablespoon soy sauce. Spread on lamb during last 10 to 15 minutes of cooking.
Italian Baste	Baste meat with dry white wine while grilling. Combine ¼ cup dry bread crumbs, 2 tablespoons Parmesan cheese, 1 clove garlic, finely chopped, ½ teaspoon basil leaves, ½ teaspoon salt and dash pepper. Pat on meat halfway through cooking time. Continue basting with wine and pat on more crumb mixture, if needed.
Mustard Dill Sauce	Combine ½ cup mayonnaise, ½ cup dairy sour cream, 2 tablespoons sliced green onion, 2 teaspoons Dijon mustard, 1 teaspoon Worcestershire sauce, 1 teaspoon dill weed, and ½ teaspoon salt. Cover; refrigerate several hours. To serve, spoon over grilled lamb.
Pineapple Chutney Sauce	In a saucepan, combine 1 can (15¼ oz.) crushed pineapple, ½ cup chutney, ¼ cup firmly packed brown sugar, ¼ cup butter, 1 teaspoon ground ginger and ½ teaspoon salt. Bring mixture to a boil; cook over low heat 5 minutes, stirring occasionally. Spread on lamb during last 10 to 15 minutes of cooking.
Seasonings	Suggested seasonings for lamb: basil leaves, rosemary leaves, thyme, garlic, ground ginger and curry powder.

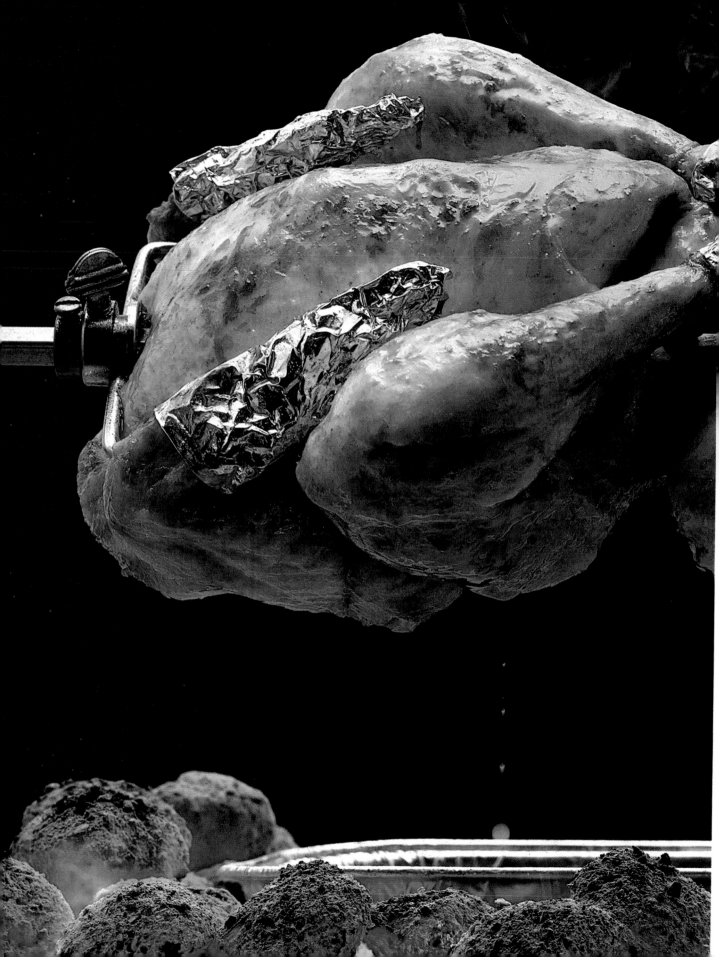

Poultry

Chicken has everything going for it: it's nutritious, low in fat and calories, and economical. But other kinds of poultry are delicious when barbecued, too.

Game hens, ducklings and turkeys all can be roasted over the coals or grilled to make great eating for family or company meals. For best results, cook poultry over medium to low coals and baste it thoroughly and often. Marinating enhances flavor and adds variety. An aluminum foil drip pan prevents burned skin, saves juices for meat gravy.

How to Smoke Poultry

Water Smoker. Smoke a turkey breast or other poultry in a water smoker. Add hickory chips to enhance flavor. Follow manufacturers' directions.

Covered Cooker. For smoked flavor in a covered cooker add hickory chips and liquid smoke to the coals. Place the poultry on grid opposite coals. Keep the cover closed and use low heat. Turn occasionally.

How to Barbecue Chicken

Covered Cooker. Grill chicken parts, quarters and halves over medium, direct heat. Cooking time will be shortened and smoked barbecued flavor will be stronger than in an open brazier.

Open Brazier. Grill chicken parts over medium, direct heat. Turn every 10 minutes to ensure even cooking.

How to Barbecue Turkey

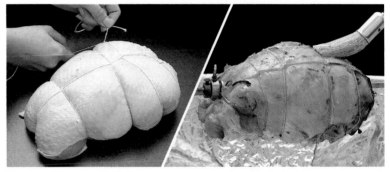

Whole Turkey. Grill in a covered cooker over indirect heat. Save time; cook two small turkeys instead of one. Brush with liquid hickory smoke.

Turkey Breast. Grill for an inexpensive low calorie, low cholesterol entrée. Thaw; tie with clean string to form an even shape, pictured above left. Thread on spit; brush with butter and baste with sauce, page 34. Roast over medium, indirect heat, pictured above right.

How to Barbecue Duck and Game Hens

Duckling. Grill over medium, indirect heat in a covered cooker. For quartered ducklings turn every 10 minutes, pictured above left. For whole ducklings score skin for self-basting and place in roasting rack, pictured above right. Brush with soy sauce for added flavor.

Game Hens. Grill over medium, indirect heat. Baste hen inside and out with herb butter. Cook breast side up, covered, with vents open. Baste often.

How to Combination-Cook Poultry

Grill twice the amount of poultry pieces you need for one meal. Freeze extras in Heavy Duty Reynolds Wrap.®

Unwrap chicken. Defrost and warm in microwave. Chicken will taste and look freshly grilled.

Reverse method. While starting coals, micro-cook larger cuts of poultry for half of recommended time. Finish on grill.

How to Bundle Wrap a Chicken Dinner

Bundle Wrap chicken in an aluminum foil packet. Remove skin for low calorie combinations; debone for an easy no mess meal; then add garden fresh vegetables with your favorite herbs or sauce. Grill over medium, direct heat 30 to 40 minutes.

Remove with tongs and open carefully. Expect steaming. Sprinkle with Parmesan cheese before serving. Serve directly from aluminum foil packet.

How to Grill Chicken in a Basket

Oil a hinged wire basket. Place chicken parts in wire basket and grill slowly over medium, direct heat. Turn every 10 minutes until finished cooking.

Baste for chicken should contain some fat to compensate for bird's leanness. Baste with barbecue sauce during last 15 minutes only to prevent burning.

58

How to Rotisserie Other Types of Poultry

Wash and season bird. Don't stuff birds to be grilled on rotisserie, just use herb butter and seasonings. Grill stuffing separately. See page 60 for directions.

Tie wings and legs securely to body to prevent flopping. Skewer neck skin to back. It's easiest to truss birds before mounting on spit.

Thread one prong onto spit and run the spit from the neck to the tail of bird. When bird is in position, insert second prong and secure tightly.

Test balance by rotating spit in hand. If bird is flopping on spit, re-thread and tighten prongs. Rotate again.

Mount several birds on one spit by butting them head to tail. Try small game hens, chicken, turkey. Be sure to tie all wings and legs. Rotate by hand for balance check. Be sure to use enough coals to cook thoroughly.

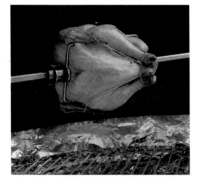

One bird balances best if spit is slightly toward backbone of bird, since breast cavity is hollow. Place bird in center of spit.

Two birds should be of similar size and shape for best balance. Poor balance will affect browning because they won't rotate smoothly on the spit.

Three or four game hens can go crosswise on spit, front-back, front-back. Butt close together for best balance. Place long, narrow aluminum foil pan under birds for drippings.

How to Cook Stuffing While Grilling Poultry

Bundle Wrap favorite stuffing in a double thickness of aluminum foil. Add several drops of water to prevent drying out.

Place aluminum foil packet on edge of grid, away from hot center of coals. Grill 15 to 20 minutes or until heated through.

Remove aluminum foil packet from grill and serve stuffing with a spoonful or two of juices from drip pan for extra flavor.

Tips for Grilling Poultry

1. Season birds for better flavor. Try hickory salt, garlic powder, paprika, pepper and parsley or your favorite combination.

2. Cook all poultry to an internal temperature of 185°F. For birds high in fat, such as duck, make certain drip pan is positioned to catch all drippings to prevent flare-ups.

3. Test poultry for doneness. Grill poultry until it is well done and flesh is no longer pink. Meat thermometer should read 185°F, and fork can be inserted with ease.

Poultry Chart

Cook all poultry over medium, indirect heat except for broiler-fryer parts and quarters, which use medium, direct heat.

Type of Poultry	Time in Covered Grill	Time on Rotisserie	Time on Open Brazier
Broiler-Fryer:			
Whole 2½ to 3½ lbs.	1¼ to 1½ hours	1½ to 2 hours	*
Parts	30 to 35 minutes	*	35 to 40 minutes
Quarters	40 to 50 minutes	*	30 to 40 minutes
Cornish Hens			
Whole 1½ lbs.	30 to 40 minutes	1 to 1½ hours	*
Domestic Duck			
Whole 4 to 5 lbs.	1¾ to 2¼ hours	2½ to 3 hours	*
Quarters	1 to 1¼ hours	*	*
Turkey			
Whole 7 to 8 lbs.	2 to 2½ hours	*	*
Whole 15 lbs.	4½ hours	*	*
Breast 5 to 6 lbs.	1½ to 2 hours	2½ to 3 hours	*

*This method not recommended.

Poultry Variations

Name/Yield	Ingredients	Method	Cooking Time
Cornish Hens 4 servings	1 pkg. (6¼ oz.) quick-cooking long grain and wild rice ½ lb. pork sausage 1 cup chopped onion ½ cup chopped celery 4 Cornish hens	Prepare rice according to package directions. Cook sausage, celery and onion together in frying pan. Drain. Combine with cooked rice. Stuff hens. Place in four Redi-Pan® Mini-Casserole Pans.	25 to 30 minutes, medium, indirect heat, in covered grill.
Grilled Duckling and a side of sauce 4 servings	1 4- to 5-lb. domestic duck 1 can (15¼ oz.) pineapple chunks, drained 1 can (11 oz.) mandarin oranges, drained 1 medium green pepper, cut into rings 1 pkg. (2 oz.) sweet and sour sauce mix ⅓ cup water 3 tablespoons vinegar	Cut duckling into quarters. Combine remaining ingredients in a Reynolds Wrap® saucepan. Spoon sauce over duckling quarters when serving.	**Duckling Quarters:** 1 to 1¼ hours, medium, indirect heat, in covered grill. **Fruit Sauce:** 20 to 30 minutes, in same grill.
Bundle-Wrapped Chicken Dinner 4 servings	8 chicken parts 2 cups sliced summer squash 4 slices cooked, crumbled bacon 2 envelopes instant single serving onion soup Dairy sour cream	Place chicken, squash and bacon on four sheets of aluminum foil. Sprinkle with soup. Bundle Wrap. Spoon sour cream over packets when serving.	40 minutes, medium, direct heat, in open brazier.
Poultry Kabobs with Stir-Fried Vegetables 4 servings	½ cup soy sauce 2 tablespoons brown sugar ¼ teaspoon ground ginger ¼ teaspoon garlic powder 4 to 5 cups fresh vegetables, bite-size chunks 4 skewers of poultry kabobs, page 75	Combine soy sauce, brown sugar, ginger and garlic. Toss half of sauce with vegetables. Stir-fry with 1 teaspoon cooking oil in Redi-Pan Lasagna Pan. Place kabobs around edge of grill. Baste with the remaining sauce.	**Vegetables:** 10 minutes, hot, direct heat, stirring frequently. **Kabobs:** 15 to 20 minutes, medium, indirect heat, turning once.
Turkey Breast with Vegetable Casserole 8 servings	1 pkg. (10 oz.) frozen broccoli spears 1 medium onion, parboiled and quartered 1 can (11 oz.) Cheddar cheese soup ¼ cup milk ½ cup soft bread crumbs 2 tablespoons melted butter	Partially defrost broccoli and cut into 1-inch pieces. Place in Redi-Pan Square Cake Pan with onion. Combine soup and milk. Add to vegetables. Top with combined bread crumbs and butter. Cover with aluminum foil.	**Turkey Breast:** 1½ to 2 hours, medium, indirect heat, in covered grill. **Casserole:** 25 to 30 minutes, medium, indirect heat. (Remove aluminum foil cover last 10 minutes.)

Fish & Seafood

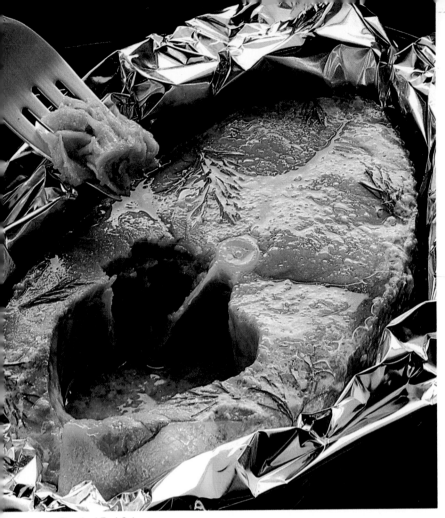

Fish

There's a way to grill every kind of fish and seafood available. Firmer fleshed fish steaks like salmon and swordfish can be marinated then grilled quickly over the coals.

Remember to support delicate fish like brook trout with a wire basket or aluminum foil loop. Larger, whole fish can be stuffed and steamed over the coals by wrapping in Heavy Duty Reynolds Wrap.® Basting enhances fish flavor. Be sure to baste lean fish, like whitefish to prevent drying. Basting is not necessary with fattier fish like bluefish or mackerel but can add flavor.

Cooking your fish to perfection is easy on the grill. Don't overcook. *Never* overhandle!

Poached Red Salmon

Grilling Time for Fish

Measure raw fish, stuffed fish or fish roll-ups at thickest point. If fish is placed 4 inches from medium-hot coals, grilling time will be in basket, on grid or in covered grill, 10 minutes per inch; if foil-wrapped, 15 minutes per inch.

How to Know if Fish is Done

Fin. Tug gently on side (pectoral) fin. If it comes away easily, fish is done. If not, grill additional 5 to 10 minutes.

Juices. If the juices run clear when fish is pricked and flesh can be flaked with fork, the fish is done.

Flesh. Fish is done when flesh is opaque and there are no traces of pinkness remaining near the backbone.

64

How to Poach Fish in Individual Aluminum Foil Packets

Tear off a sheet of Heavy Duty Reynolds Wrap® large enough for adequate wrapping; grease. Place ½- to ¾-pound small whole fish, steak or single layer of fillets on aluminum foil.

Season fish with salt, pepper, paprika and parsley. Combine 2 tablespoons water, 1 tablespoon melted butter and 1 tablespoon lemon juice or dry white wine; pour over fish.

Seal with Bundle Wrap, page 29. Place 4 to 5 inches over medium-hot coals. Cook according to Grilling Time, page 64.

How to Bake Fish in Aluminum Foil Packets

Grease center of sheet of heavy duty aluminum foil. Place a layer of sliced lemon on center of aluminum foil. Top lemon slices with whole fish, fish steaks or fish fillets.

Season fish with celery salt, pepper, onion powder, parsley and melted butter. If desired, layer fillets or stuff cavity of whole fish with sliced or shredded vegetables.

Seal with Drugstore Wrap, page 29. Place packet 4 to 5 inches over medium-hot coals. Cook according to Grilling Time, page 64.

How to Stuff and Cook Whole Fish

Clean and dress fish. Rub inside with seasonings. Fill fish loosely with seasoned bread or rice stuffing. Bind with clean string or foil loops, page 67. Cook using covered grill or the open brazier method.

Covered Grill Method. Place in greased Reynolds Wrap® baking pan, page 19. Top with melted butter and lemon slices. Cook in covered grill over medium-hot coals according to Grilling Time, page 64.

Open Brazier Method. Drugstore Wrap fish to cook on open brazier. Cook over medium-hot coals according to Grilling Time, page 64.

Baked Fish with Vegetables

How to Grill Fish in Hinged Grill Basket

Use a long-handled hinged grill basket for grilling more delicate fillets, steaks and small whole fish. Basket will make turning easier and faster.

Season or marinate fish for 30 minutes before grilling. Place in oiled wire basket. Brush with marinade or melted butter; top one side with thin lemon slice.

Place basket with fish 4 to 5 inches over medium-hot coals. Sear one side and turn to finish. Brush with marinade or melted butter during cooking to prevent drying.

How to Grill Fish in Flat Spit Basket

Clean small whole fish. Leave skin on. Season cavity of fish with melted butter, salt, pepper and herbs.

Oil a flat spit basket with vegetable oil or oil-based salad dressing. Gently lay fish side-by-side in basket. Close basket tightly, being careful not to crush fish.

Center basket on spit. Basket should be directly over medium-hot coals at rotisserie height. Turn on rotisserie; baste fish once during cooking.

Fish Recipe Chart

Type	Method
Stuffing for Whole Fish	To add additional flavor and zest to whole fish, fill cavity with lemon herb stuffing. Prepare herb-seasoned stuffing mix according to package directions. Add parsley, grated lemon peel, basil and garlic to taste. Top stuffed fish with melted butter, lemon juice and thinly sliced onion rings. To grill see page 65.
Baked Fish with Vegetables	Sprinkle cavity of whole fish with salt and pepper. Tie with clean string. Place in greased aluminum foil pan. Sauté sliced onion and chopped garlic in butter; add basil leaves, parsley and chopped fresh or canned and drained tomatoes or favorite sliced vegetable. Pour over fish. Top with cooked, crumbled bacon. Cook in covered grill 4 to 5 inches over medium-hot coals.
Baked Fish with Herbs and Lemon	Salt and pepper fish steaks, fillets or whole fish. Place fish on heavy duty aluminum foil. Sprinkle with dill weed, or favorite herb, chopped green onion and 1 tablespoon sherry or melted butter. Top with sliced lemon. Seal with Drugstore Wrap, page 29. Cook on grid 4 to 5 inches over medium-hot coals.

How to Make Reynolds Wrap Loops

Tear off a 12-inch length of Heavy Duty Reynolds Wrap.® Fold in half lengthwise four times to make a strip ¾ inch wide. Grease one side of strip and place under fish.

Fold in half with ends meeting above the fish. Fold ends together in locked folds until snug against fish.

Twist once to secure loop and form handle for turning. Turn fish over with mitts, using loop handles. (Use one loop for fish steaks and two for large fish.)

How to Grill Fish Directly on Grid

Select firm-fleshed and sturdy-skinned whole fish or fish steaks to grill directly on grid. Marinate fish steaks 30 minutes before cooking, if desired. Wrap loops around fish.

Oil grid generously. Place fish 4 to 5 inches over medium-hot coals. Use covered or brazier grill. Brush with marinade or melted butter during cooking.

Turn fish with Reynolds Wrap loops halfway through cooking time. Cook according to Grilling Time, page 64.

Shellfish

If you have access to fresh seafood, your barbecue pleasures are multiplied. Seafood requires little in the way of pre-preparation and takes very little time over the coals. It's appetizing when cooked "au natural" and rises to sublime heights when marinated and/or sauced. You can serve seafood appetizers before a main course of beef or chicken or make a meal of a mixed seafood grill. If the big grill is busy cooking roast, why not bring out an extra hibachi or portable grill and let guests toast their own shrimp or crab legs?

Shrimp

Place six medium cleaned shrimp on Heavy Duty Reynolds Wrap.® Sprinkle with salt and pepper, add 2 tablespoons Garlic Butter, page 35. Bundle Wrap. Grill over medium, direct heat 10 to 12 minutes.

Butterfly a larger shrimp or use smaller shelled deveined whole shrimp. Grill over low coals until pink and firm, about 5 minutes. Brush often with marinade. Do not overcook.

Mussels

Scrub beards from small mussels. Soak in cold water in refrigerator 1 hour. Place knob of garlic butter on square of heavy duty aluminum foil.

Add single layer of six mussels to aluminum foil. Bundle Wrap. Grill 4 inches from medium-hot coals, shaking bundle often. When mussels open, serve at once with garlic butter.

Clams and Oysters

Scrub shells of clams and oysters well. Soak in salt water. Rinse well in cold water.

Place clams and oysters directly on grid over medium-high coals. Cook until shells just begin to open.

Turn and grill for an additional 5 to 15 minutes or until the clams and oysters pop open. Do not overcook.

Lobster and Crab

Lobster. Place live lobster head first into rapidly boiling water. Remove when water re-boils. Split and clean, pictured above left. Brush with herb butter. Grill 3 inches from medium coals, shell down, for about 10 minutes. Turn and grill for an additional 5 minutes or until done, pictured above right.

Crab. Defrost King crab legs. Split; remove top half of shell. Baste with Italian dressing. Grill flesh up 5 inches from medium heat 10 minutes. Turn and grill 5 more minutes or until done.

Rock Lobster Tails

Thaw lobster tails before grilling. Snip off thin shell on flesh side. Bend backward to crack shell in several places.

Baste with butter. Place shell side down on grill. Barbecue 10 minutes, basting often.

Turn and grill 5 minutes more until flesh is opaque and flakes easily. Serve with lemon and melted butter.

Smoking Fish and Shellfish

Smoking does more than add flavor, it makes seafood delightfully firm. Fish can be dry smoked in a kettle or slowly smoked in a water smoker grill. Smoke whole fish, chunks, steaks and fillets. Vary flavor with aromatic liquids like beer and wine, and with favorite herbs. As with regular grilling, it's a good idea to line the fire pan with Heavy Duty Reynolds Wrap® to create an even heat distribution and ease cleanup. Follow the manufacturer's directions that come with your water smoker for arranging food, coals and water pan.

How to Smoke Oysters and Clams

Open clams or oysters with special round-blade knife. Drain out liquid; leave in half shell.

Arrange clams and oysters in the half shell on grid. Season to taste. Squeeze on lime or lemon juice for tang.

Smoke-cook 1 to 2 hours or until flesh is set. Time varies with the size of the shellfish.

How to Smoke Fish in a Water Smoker

Mix 1 quart water with ¼ cup Kosher salt until dissolved. Pour into glass or plastic container. Add 2 to 3 pounds fish fillets, steaks or pan-dressed fish. Chill 4 hours or overnight.

Air-dry fish on wire racks at least 30 minutes before cooking. Fish should be dry to the touch before grilling.

Burn charcoal fire at least 30 minutes before adding dampened hickory or fruitwood chips. Add more coals every hour to maintain gentle heat.

Fill water pan of smoker as manufacturer directs. Always use hot water to maintain temperature. If you like, add aromatic herbs and liquids.

Coat grid with oil to prevent sticking. Place fish apart in single layer. For small pieces cover grid with aluminum foil and punch holes to allow for steam.

Grill ¾- to 1-inch thick fillets 2 to 2½ hours. Reduce time for smaller fish. Fish is done when it flakes with fork. Serve smoked fish in salad or as an appetizer.

How to Smoke Fish in a Covered Grill

Soak hickory chips in water at least 30 minutes. Place charcoal briquets in one side of grill. Light briquets and let burn to ash covered stage. Add drained hickory chips to briquets.

Soak fish at least 30 minutes in saltwater mixture. Air-dry fish. Fish should be dry to the touch. Brush with cooking oil.

Place fish on grid opposite coals. Cover grill and partially close vents to keep heat low. Cook 30 to 45 minutes or until fish flakes.

Kabobs

Plan ingredients for a kabob cookout with an idea of what flavors complement each other. Set up skewers so that when juices intermingle, new interesting flavors result. Most basic skewers are stainless steel; use potholders or mitts to turn these. Better yet are two-pronged or square skewers, since they prevent flopping. For good function, use skewers with wooden handles which are easy to hold and turn. Use more than one kind of marinade in a meal.

How to Prepare Food for Skewers

Chunks. Cut meats and vegetables into bite-size chunks or rounds for easiest handling.

Strips. Weave meat strips 1 inch wide and ¼ inch thick onto skewer accordion-style. Place fruits and vegetables in loops. Turn kabobs frequently.

Wedges. Use sweet onions, green peppers, eggplant, potatoes, cantaloupe and fresh pineapple. Tuck the smaller cut wedges into larger ones.

Whole Foods. They retain identity, have eye appeal. Skewer scallops, cocktail franks, cherry tomatoes and whole mushrooms.

Tips for Kabob-ing

Parboil slower cooking foods so grilling times will be same as other foods on the skewer. Parboil small white onions, carrots and chunks of corn-on-the-cob.

Stuff centers of pork and beef balls with water chestnuts, mushrooms, olives or pineapple for best results. Select stuffing, work into center of meatball, then skewer.

Serve individual skewers of meat or vegetables as an appetizer. Soak wooden skewers briefly in water. Assemble food on skewer. Marinate, turning once. Grill.

Prepare separate skewers of vegetables so that they will not be overcooked when grilling chunks of meat and poultry at the same time.

Wrap cooked kabob skewers in Heavy Duty Reynolds Wrap® to keep warm until serving time.

Marinate 3 to 4 hours to ensure tenderness for economical, less tender cuts of meat.

Kabob Chart

Type	Time, direct heat	Method
Beef		
Sirloin	Medium-hot	Grill, turning frequently.
1½-inch cubes	12 to 14 minutes	
¼-inch strips	8 to 10 minutes	
Round		
1½-inch cubes	8 to 12 minutes	Marinate 3 to 4 hours in Beer Marinade, page 33. Grill, turning frequently.
Chuck		
1¼- to 1½-inch cubes	10 to 12 minutes	Same as above.

Kabob Chart, Continued

Type	Time, direct heat	Method
Ground Beef		
Stuffed meatballs - 1½-inch	Medium-hot 18 to 20 minutes	Use water chestnuts, whole mushrooms, pickles or olives as center of meatball. Turn often.
Fish and Seafood		
Shrimp green, peeled, deveined (medium size)	Medium 4 to 5 minutes	Grill, turning often. Brush with melted butter seasoned with lemon and garlic.
Scallops		Same as above.
Fruit		
Cubes	Medium 5 to 8 minutes	Grill until warm but not brown. Baste with Cinnamon Butter or a sauce, page 34, 35.
Lamb		
Leg or Shoulder 1¼-inch cubes	Medium 13 to 16 minutes	Marinate 3 to 4 hours in Apple Tarragon Marinade, page 33. Grill, turning frequently.
Pork		
Loin 1¼-inch cubes	Medium-low 15 to 18 minutes	Grill, turning frequently. Brush with Hot and Spicy Sauce, page 34, during last 10 minutes of cooking time.
Shoulder 1¼-inch cubes	14 to 16 minutes	Marinate 3 to 4 hours in Pineapple Marinade, page 33. Grill, turning frequently.
Ground Pork		
Stuffed meatballs 1½-inch	Medium-hot 15 to 17 minutes	Use water chestnuts, green pepper chunks or pineapple chunks as center of meatball. Grill, turning often. Brush with bottled Teriyaki sauce.
Poultry		
Chicken 1-inch chunks ¼-inch strips	Medium-hot 15 to 18 minutes 13 to 15 minutes	Grill, turning frequently. Brush with melted butter or marinate in Teriyaki Marinade, page 33.
Chicken livers	8 to 10 minutes	Thread with bacon strips. Grill. Turn often.
Turkey 1¼- to 1½-inch chunks	18 to 20 minutes	Grill. Turn often. Brush with melted butter, season with salt, pepper and paprika before serving or brush with Hot and Spicy Sauce, page 34, during last 10 minutes of cooking.
Sausage		
Polish sausage ¾-inch cubes	Medium 13 to 15 minutes	Grill, turning often.
Bratwurst ¾-inch cubes	15 to 18 minutes	Grill, turning often.
Vegetables		Refer to Vegetable Chart, page 83

Game

Preparation of wild game is not very different from other meats. The difference lies in the fact that wild game offers more variety. There is a fuller flavor, the meat is lean and often drier than domestic. This varies with the cooking method, age and variety of the game.

The meat should be marinated and tenderized before cooking. Sportsmen know there is no better way to cook small game than roasted over the coals. The smoky charcoal flavor is a perfect match for the stronger flavor of some wild animals. Some small game like wild mallard and rabbit, are delicious when cooked in a water smoker. Serve instant rice with almonds, page 81, a pilaf made in a Reynolds Wrap saucepan alongside the meat.

If desired, game can be Drugstore Wrapped in Heavy Duty Reynolds Wrap,® labeled and frozen for later use.

Some wild game, like quail and pheasant, tend to be dry and benefit from bacon wrapped around the skin or basting with bacon drippings during cooking. For directions see pages 77 and 78.

Venison has a very distinct flavor, similar to young beef. Because it is very lean, it benefits from marinating and from frequent basting during cooking with an oily marinade. The slow, moist roasting of a water smoker is ideal for venison because it keeps the meat tender and juicy.

How to Barbecue Rabbit

Marinate rabbit overnight in refrigerator in red wine marinade. Add natural liquid hickory smoke for outdoor flavor.

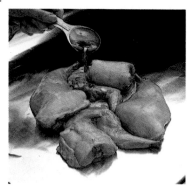

Place rabbit on large sheet of heavy duty aluminum foil. Add 2 tablespoons of the marinade.

Seal packet with Bundle Wrap. Place on grill over medium, direct heat. Grill about 1 hour or until rabbit is done.

How to Barbecue Quail

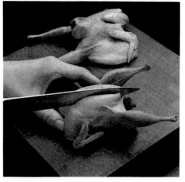

Barbecue fresh quail for optimum flavor. Clean and split birds lengthwise. Allow one to two birds per person.

Brush quail with butter and place skin side down on grid over medium, direct heat. Grill 5 minutes, or until browned.

Turn. Brush generously with butter or bacon fat. Grill an additional 5 to 7 minutes.

How to Barbecue Whole Wild Duck

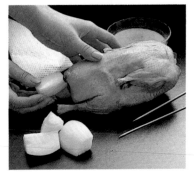

Wipe duck inside and out with damp cloth. Place piece of apple or onion in cavity. Skewer closed. Brush with melted Parsley Orange Butter, page 35.

Truss birds same as for chicken. Cook breast side up in covered grill over indirect, low heat. Place aluminum foil drip pan under duck.

Baste frequently with melted butter. Cook small ducks (about 1½ lbs. each) for about 1 hour or until meat thermometer registers 185°F.

How to Barbecue Pheasant

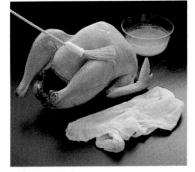

Wipe pheasant inside and out with a damp cloth. Brush outside of bird generously with butter since pheasant has a tendency to be very dry.

Wrap pheasant all around with strips of bacon. Season with freshly ground pepper. Cook on roasting rack in covered grill over medium, indirect heat.

Remove bacon during last 15 minutes to brown. If legs and wing tips look dry cover with foil. Cook 1 to 1¼ hours. Meat thermometer registers 185°F.

How to Grill Whole Goose

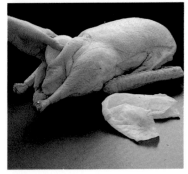

Wipe goose inside and out with a damp cloth. Place piece of apple or onion in cavity. Truss the bird.

Brush with melted butter rosemary, thyme, salt and pepper. Place on roast rack.

Cook in covered grill over indirect, low heat. Place drip pan under goose. Cook 1½ to 2 hours or until meat thermometer registers 185°F.

How to Prepare Venison Steaks

Marinate venison steak in White Wine Marinade, page 33. Cover and refrigerate overnight. Turn occasionally.

Drain and season. Sear quickly on both sides over medium, direct heat until medium-rare, pictured above left. Or, cut steak into 1¼-inch cubes. Marinate 3 hours, skewer and grill over medium, direct heat until medium-rare, pictured above right.

How to Prepare Venison Roast

Remove fat and second skin from 3- to 4-pound loin roast. Season; use White Wine Marinade, page 33. Cover; refrigerate overnight. Turn occasionally.

Cook on covered grill using medium to low, indirect heat. Cook to an internal temperature of 160°F for medium doneness or 140°F for rare.

To serve, slice roast thinly, across the grain. Serve sliced roast with stuffed onion or stuffed tomato, page 85.

Vegetables

Experiment with grilling and you will develop some vegetable specialties. Favorite recipes for the range and oven can be done in a covered grill if you allow extra time for baking. Vegetables buttered, seasoned and wrapped in Heavy Duty Reynolds Wrap® then grilled, retain wonderful steamed-in flavor and have an appealing barely cooked texture.

There are five basic methods for grilling vegetables: ember cooking, foil wrapping, directly on grid, skewered, and stir-fried. Try any one of these methods on an open grill, in a covered unit or in a charcoal water smoker.

How to Foil Wrap

Drugstore Wrap potatoes or similar vegetables. Place on edge of grid on a covered grill while cooking a roast. Turn potatoes several times while cooking. To serve, cut open and add desired topping.

Bundle Wrap a variety of vegetables. As a side dish for your favorite steak, Bundle Wrap individual servings of onions, mushrooms, green peppers and seasonings. Use medium, direct heat.

Reynolds Wrap saucepan is ideal for rice almondine. Boil water, salt and butter in saucepan. Add same amount of instant rice as water. Add almonds. Cover tightly with aluminum foil. Serve when water is absorbed. Keep warm on grill.

How to Ember Cook

Ember cook hard vegetables like acorn squash and sweet potatoes right in coals, with or without a foil wrap. Oil the skins before placing in coals.

Foil Wrap more delicately skinned vegetables. For corn, remove the silk, keeping the husk. Soak in ice water and Drugstore Wrap. Turn frequently for even cooking.

Drugstore Wrap is desirable for ember cooking since it permits turning. To prevent charring chunked vegetables like zucchini, green peppers, or onions, wrap in double thickness of heavy duty aluminum foil.

Stuffed potatoes, page 85

How to Skewer Cook Vegetables

Cut vegetables into bite-size wedges or chunks. Alternate shapes for variety. The thinner the vegetable is cut, the more quickly it will cook.

Skewer vegetables alternating with meat chunks or strips. Strips of beef can shield more delicate vegetables like tomatoes and mushrooms. Brush with soy/teriyaki sauce and grill.

All vegetable skewers should be threaded with similar sizes and shapes of vegetables to promote more even cooking. Skewer zucchini and yellow squash; mushrooms and green peppers; onions and potatoes; sweet potatoes and pineapple.

How to Grill Directly on Grid

Parboil root vegetables and cook directly on the grid over medium coals turning frequently. Baste with seasoned butter.

Halve summer squash lengthwise, brush with butter and grill in hinged basket. Oil basket to prevent sticking. Grill over medium, direct heat 15 to 20 minutes. Turn frequently.

Cover cut edge of halved vegetables with Heavy Duty Reynolds Wrap® to prevent charring. Grill cut side down first. Turn halfway through cooking time.

How to Stir Fry Over the Coals

Place large wok directly over the coals or on grid over coals. Use ring for balance. Some grills come with wok that fits directly into grill. Use long-handled tongs or wooden spoon to stir quickly.

Use a Redi-Pan® Lasagna Pan if a wok is not available. Set pan on grid over hot coals, add small amount of oil and stir vegetables until tender but crisp. Season with soy sauce.

Vegetable Chart

Vegetable	Method	Preparation	Seasoning	Time/Min.	Direct Heat
Beans, Green	Drugstore Wrap	Cut diagonally.	Almonds, butter and a few tablespoons water	20 to 25	medium
Carrots	Drugstore Wrap	Scrub, don't peel. Discard ends.	Butter, basil and a few tablespoons water	25	medium
	On grid	Parboil 3 minutes.	Herbed butter	35 to 40	medium-low
Corn Whole	*Ember	Remove silk, leaving husk. Soak in water.	—	35 to 45	low, turn often
	Drugstore Wrap	Remove husks and silk.	Butter, salt, pepper and a few tablespoons water	45	medium
Cut	Bundle Wrap	Cut corn off cob.	Chopped onion, green pepper and tomato	20	medium
Chunks	Kabobs	Parboil 3 minutes.	Melted butter	5 to 10	medium
Eggplant	Bundle Wrap	Slice.	Butter, Parmesan cheese and sliced tomatoes.	15	medium
Mushrooms	Bundle Wrap	Cut off stems.	Butter, salt and pepper	15 to 20	medium
	Kabobs	Cut off stems.	Melted butter	6 to 8	medium
Onions	*Ember	Remove ends.	—	45	low, turn often
	Kabobs	Parboil 3 minutes.	Melted butter	20	medium
Peppers	Kabobs	Cut in 1½-inch chunks.	Melted butter	12 to 15	medium
Potatoes, Sweet or Baking	*Ember Drugstore Wrap	Oil whole vegetable.	—	45 to 55 55 to 60	low, turn often low
Halves	On grid	Cover cut sides with aluminum foil.	—	60	medium, turn once
Slices	Bundle Wrap	Slice very thin. Spread in even layer.	Butter, salt, pepper	45	medium-hot
Cubes	Kabobs	Peeled, 1¼-inch.	Melted butter	35 to 40	medium-hot
New	On grid	Scrub.	Melted butter	40 to 50	medium
Summer Squash	Bundle Wrap	Slices, lengthwise.	Salt, pepper and butter	20	medium
	Kabobs	1¼-inch chunks.	Italian salad dressing	12 to 15	medium
	Grill basket	Slices, lengthwise.	Melted butter	15 to 20	medium
Tomatoes, Halves	Bundle Wrap	Cut in half.	Butter, Parmesan cheese and parsley	30 to 40	medium
Cherry	Kabobs	Leave whole.	Melted butter.	5	medium
Winter Squash,	*Ember	Oil whole vegetables.	—	45 to 55	low, turn often
Halves	Grid	Cover cut sides with aluminum foil.	—	60	medium, turn once.

*Ember cook — wrap vegetables in heavy duty aluminum foil or place directly on coals.

Stuffed Vegetable Meals

For optimum results, wrap stuffed vegetables in aluminum foil and cook in a covered grill. However, foil wrapped vegetables can be cooked on an open grill but will require additional time.

How to Stuff Eggplant

Cut tops lengthwise from two eggplants. Scoop out insides of eggplants, leaving ½-inch wall. Place shells on sheet of Heavy Duty Reynolds Wrap.®

Chop pulp of eggplants; sauté in butter with onion, zucchini, tomatoes, garlic and olives. Combine with cooked rice and spaghetti sauce.

Spoon into eggplant shells. Drugstore Wrap. Cook over medium, indirect heat in a covered grill 35 minutes or until heated through.

How to Stuff Vegetables

Stuffed Green Pepper. Cut off top of green pepper; clean. Fill with cooked bulgur wheat, chopped pecans, tomatoes, tomato paste, garlic powder, basil leaves, mozzarella cheese, sautéed mushrooms and onions. Bundle Wrap in aluminum foil. Cook in covered grill over medium, indirect heat 35 minutes.

Stuffed Tomato. Hollow out; drain. Fill with frozen peas, slightly thawed, green onion, Parmesan cheese, salt, pepper and melted butter. Bundle Wrap. Cook in a covered grill over medium, indirect heat 35 minutes.

Stuffed Sweet Onion. Hollow out. Fill with frozen spinach soufflé, slightly thawed. Bundle Wrap. Cook in a covered grill over medium, indirect heat 50 minutes. Open packet during last 5 minutes.

Stuffed Potato. Slit potato at ¼-inch intervals. Do not cut all the way through. Place onion slices, seasoned salt, garlic powder, celery salt, pepper and butter in slits. Top with sliced mushrooms. Drugstore Wrap. Grill over hot, direct heat 55 to 60 minutes. To serve, open packet and top with cooked bacon, Parmesan cheese, tomatoes and parsley.

Stuffed Butternut Squash. Cut squash in half. Remove seeds. Combine cooked and crumbled pork sausage, seasoned stuffing mix (prepared according to package directions), chopped onion, apple and thyme leaves. Spoon into squash. Drugstore Wrap. Cook in a covered grill over medium, indirect heat 50 minutes.

Stuffed Yellow Squash. Hollow out. Chop pulp; sauté in butter with onion, garlic and chopped spinach. Mix with mozzarella and Parmesan cheese. Spoon into squash. Drugstore Wrap. Cook in a covered grill over medium, indirect heat 20 minutes.

Breads & Desserts

When grilling breads and desserts, the use of a covered grill increases your menu options. The cover provides the same baking process as an indoor oven. If your grill does not have a cover, see page 18 for instructions on how to make an aluminum foil hood for your grill.

Use Heavy Duty Reynolds Wrap® or disposable foilware to make cooking and handling foods like breads and desserts more convenient. The aluminum foil can be used as a wrap for foods with either a Bundle or Drugstore Wrap, as a baking pan or as a serving container. Since coals will be at low heat

by the time you are ready to grill dessert, be sure to bank them all together before grilling dessert. For best results when baking breads and desserts, grill with the cover down. This provides an even cooking temperature and holds heat in.

The foil-wrapped loaf has many variations from grilled garlic bread to a savory herb dilled bread. For added interest, serve these breads with some of the seasoned butters listed on page 35. For brunch barbecues, serve cornbread straight from the grill, page 89. Pre-baked breads and frozen rolls are another convenient barbecue

menu addition. Foil wrap them according to the directions on page 29.

Desserts on the grill can range from skewered fruit brushed with honey and lemon to barbecued brownies, gingerbread to peanut butter cookies. Old-fashioned s'mores can be made conveniently and in advance for a traditional barbecue favorite with children. Simply sandwich a chocolate square and marshmallow creme between two graham crackers. Drugstore Wrap in heavy duty aluminum foil and grill until chocolate is melted.

How to Grill Pre-Baked Bread

Garlic Bread. Slash a loaf of French or Italian bread almost through in ¾-inch intervals. Spread garlic butter between slices. Drugstore Wrap in aluminum foil. Grill 20 minutes over medium-hot coals; turn often.

Herb Loaf. Or slash loaf as described and spread with your favorite sandwich spread. Add cheese, ham, tuna or chicken salad. Drugstore Wrap in aluminum foil. Grill 20 minutes over medium-hot coals; turn often.

Brown-and-Serve Rolls. Place rolls in Redi-Pan®. Bake in covered grill over medium-low, indirect heat 4 to 5 minutes or until evenly browned.

Assorted refrigerator biscuits and rolls

How to Barbecue Refrigerator Biscuits and Rolls

Open a can of refrigerator biscuits or rolls and separate.

Place 1 inch apart in Redi-Pan® Cake Pan. Do not grease pan.

Cover. Bake over medium-low, indirect heat 15 to 20 minutes or until crusted and done throughout.

Muffins in a Covered Grill

Prepare muffin mix according to package directions.

Grease a Redi-Pan Muffin Pan. Fill cups half full.

Grill in covered grill over medium, indirect heat for 10 to 15 minutes or until done.

How to Make Cornbread on the Grill

Use a cornbread mix to save time. Prepare, following package directions.

Pour into Redi-Pan® Square Cake Pan and set on grill using indirect heat method and medium coals.

Bake in covered grill approximately 35 minutes until cornbread pulls away from sides of pan. Cut into squares.

How to Bake Frozen Bread Loaf

Remove bread from freezer. Place in greased Redi-Pan Loaf Pan. Cover loosely and thaw in refrigerator overnight.

Let rise at room temperature until risen 1 inch above the sides of the pan.

Bake in covered grill 15 to 20 minutes over medium, indirect heat. Bake just until well browned. Turn out of pan; keep warm.

Sandwich Chart

Type	Method
Stuffed Stromboli	Cut ¼ inch off top of Kaiser roll. Hollow out center. Stuff with layers of salami, Provolone cheese, pepperoni and sautéed green pepper and onion. Cover with top. Drugstore Wrap in aluminum foil. Grill over medium coals, turning frequently until heated through.
Grilled Open-Faced Sandwich	Butter both sides of slice of pumpernickel bread. Spread top side with Dijon mustard. Layer with corned beef, finely chopped onion, caraway seeds and Swiss cheese. Place in Redi-Pan or Reynolds Wrap baking pan, page 19. Place on covered grill. Cook over medium coals until heated through.
Pocket Bread Sandwiches	Marinate beef strips in Teriyaki Marinade, page 33. Weave beef strips around green pepper chunks and thick wedges of onion and thread on skewers. Grill according to Kabob Chart, page 74. Cut ½ inch off top of pocket bread. Seal with Drugstore Wrap; place on grill until heated through. To serve, empty skewers into pocket bread.
Ham and Cheese Loaf	Cut French bread loaf diagonally at ¾-inch intervals, almost to bottom crust. Combine ½ cup butter, softened, ½ cup grated Cheddar cheese, 1 cup finely chopped ham, 1 teaspoon celery seed and 2 tablespoons chopped onion; spread filling between slices. Drugstore Wrap in aluminum foil. Grill over medium-hot coals, 20 minutes or until heated through; turn often.

Hot from the Grill Desserts

Baked Apple. Core apples. Fill with raisins, coconut, brown sugar, and cinnamon. Bundle Wrap. Grill over medium, direct coals 20 minutes until tender.

Pineapple Kabobs. Pare and cut fresh pineapple into wedges. Thread on skewers and grill over medium heat 15 minutes basting with a combination of honey, butter and cinnamon.

Pie. Heat a freshly made fruit crisp or pie in a covered grill. Prepare in aluminum foilware pan. Overwrap by using Bundle Wrap and grill over coals until steaming. Serve warm with ice cream.

Gingerbread. Prepare gingerbread mix according to package directions. Pour into ungreased Redi-Pan® Square Cake Pan. Bake in covered grill over medium, indirect coals 30 minutes. Serve with lemon sauce.

Lemon Sauce. In a Reynolds Wrap saucepan, page 19, heat your favorite lemon sauce over medium-hot, direct coals 20 minutes, stirring until thickened. Serve over gingerbread or with fresh fruit as a fondue.

Peanut Butter Cookies. Prepare one roll of refrigerator cookies. Place on ungreased Redi-Pan Cookie Sheet. Bake in covered grill over medium-low, direct heat 8 to 10 minutes. Check occasionally.

Appetizers & Snacks

Barbecued appetizers and snacks are the perfect thing to serve while guests relax before dinner or as a late night snack around the fireplace. They can be prepared with almost any type of barbecue grill. Water smokers adapt especially well to snack foods. Try smoking nuts or a small fish in a water smoker. Follow the manufacturer's directions.

Grill baskets work well with small foods like miniature chicken wings and simplify turning many small pieces at one time.

For late night snacking, try nachos over the coals. Prepare according to directions below. Many convenience foods like frozen egg rolls can be done in a covered grill. Experiment with some of your favorites. Check package directions.

How to Grill Appetizers and Snacks

Popcorn. Place 3 tablespoons popping corn and 1 tablespoon oil in center of a double thickness of heavy duty aluminum foil. Bundle Wrap, leaving expansion room. Grill over hot, direct heat; shake with long-handled tongs until popping stops.

Nachos. Place corn tortilla chips on a Redi-Pan® Toaster Oven Tray. Top with chopped green chili peppers and Monterey Jack cheese. Cover with aluminum foil tent. Grill over medium, direct heat until melted, 10 to 12 minutes.

Barbecued Party Wings. Remove and discard bony tips of chicken wings. Marinate in Teriyaki Marinade, page 33, then grill slowly in grill basket 45 minutes or until crusty brown. Terrific finger food!

Smoked Fish Log. Combine 1 pound smoked fish, page 70, flaked, 1 package (8 oz.) cream cheese, 2 tablespoons grated onion, 1 tablespoon lemon juice, 1 teaspoon prepared horseradish and ¼ teaspoon salt. Shape into a log. Wrap in aluminum foil; chill. Roll in ½ cup each chopped parsley and chopped pecans before serving.

Oysters and Clams. Shuck and drain, then place in deep halves of shells. Prepare favorite clam stuffing. Grill over hot, direct coals 12 to 15 minutes or until bubbly.

Smoked Fish Log, above.

Planning Your Event

Advance planning is essential for the success of your barbecue. The goal: everything's ready to be served at the same time, and cleanup is fast and easy. Make a time plan to accomplish this. Be realistic about how much time each chore will take. (For instance, it takes three times as long to clean 3 pounds of beans as it does to clean 1 pound.) Then schedule jobs alternately so one item is heating (or chilling) while you prepare another. A good idea is to prepare dishes that have to be chilled first. Have all items to be grilled prepared (marinated, seasoned, cut and wrapped) before the fire is ready. Be sure to allow enough time for coals to reach the best cooking temperature. Estimate and overlap cooking times of meats and vegetables so they'll be done at the same time. Study the time plan at right, based on the menu below. If you are inexperienced, you might want to allow more time for each task.

Menu

Crisp Vegetable Relishes   Sour Cream Onion Dip

Boneless Beef Roast, page 41

Foil-Wrapped Baked Potatoes, page 28   Corn Roasted in Husks, page 28

Green Beans with Almonds, page 83   Garlic Bread, page 87

Fruit Pie, page 90

Milk   Coffee

Making a Time Plan

The day before:

Check out party area, tableware. Shop.
Prepare crisp vegetable relishes. Wrap in paper towel, and overwrap in aluminum foil; chill.

The morning of:

Line grill with heavy duty aluminum foil. Prepare drip pan. Place charcoal briquets in fire pan.

3 hours before:

Make garlic butter; cover and refrigerate. Prepare dip; chill. Wash, oil and wrap potatoes. Drugstore Wrap prepared green beans.

2½ hours before:

Prepare fruit pie, baking in Redi-Pan in kitchen oven. Remove silks from corn. For 6-pound roast, light fire. When coals turn grey, put meat on grill.

2 hours before:

Set table. Soak corn in ice water. Dress for party.

1¼ hours before:

Place foil-wrapped potatoes on grid. Shake off excess water from corn; foil-wrap. Place on grid. Turn every 10 minutes. Prepare garlic bread and foil-wrap.

½ hour before (when guests have arrived):

Add more coals to fire. Turn potatoes and corn. Add green beans and garlic bread to grid. Set out vegetable relishes and dip.

¼ hour before:

Remove roast to carving board to "set." Turn corn, potatoes, garlic bread and beans. Start warming fruit pie. Heat butter to brush on corn in small Redi-Pan at side of grill.

Dinner time:

Serve corn. Place other food in suitable serving dishes and keep warm in foil wraps. Pass beverages. Start coffee to serve with dessert.

Complete Grill Meals

Entire meals, from appetizers through dessert, can be cooked over charcoal as successfully as one or two foods. For success, take into consideration both grill size and the cooking time required for such food.

For quick, refreshing summer meals, complement hot, grilled foods with cool, crisp salads and chilled fruit desserts and beverages. Continue barbecuing into fall with grilled meats, baked vegetable dishes and warm desserts. As always, plan in advance for best results.

Family Barbecue

Don't wait for company to bring out the grill. Barbecue your family's favorite foods and notice the taste difference. Give each family member a job, and the meal will be ready in no time. Assign one person to line the grill and start the fire, while others prepare the food. Clean-up will be the easy job if the grill is lined with aluminum foil and the food is cooked in aluminum foil-made saucepans and aluminum foil wraps.

Barbecue chicken, page 57, for a sure-to-please family favorite. Start longer cooking whole broiler-fryers first over medium, indirect heat in a covered grill. If an open brazier is used, choose chicken parts and grill over medium, direct heat.

Heat baked beans alongside the chicken in a Reynolds Wrap® saucepan, page 19. Stir and cook until heated through.

Grill tomato halves, summer squash or whole carrots, Bundle Wrapped, page 83. Time the vegetables to be done simultaneously with the chicken.

Place refrigerator rolls or biscuits on the covered grill using medium-low, indirect heat, 15 to 20 minutes. Serve with honey and butter.

Serve gingerbread and lemon sauce, page 91 for dessert. Use Heavy Duty Reynolds Wrap® and disposable aluminum foilware to avoid any major cleanup after the meal.

Pig Roast

Plan a pig roast for an unusual way to feed a large crowd. Two weeks ahead, order a dressed pig, split down the backbone. Plan on 1½ pounds of dressed pig per person. One week ahead, locate heavy grating for the grid no smaller than 3 × 4½ ft. or 6 inches larger than pig. Locate steel reinforcing rods for the hood. Do not use galvanized or soldered metal or metal containing lead. Buy two 100-ft. rolls of Heavy Duty Reynolds Wrap® for easy cleanup and even heat distribution. One day ahead, build the pit and prepare your favorite basting sauce. Try a tomato-based sauce for a Southern barbecue or a sweet and sour sauce for a Hawaiian luau. Serve with ember cooked potatoes and winter squash, page 81, pineapple kabobs, page 90 and your favorite fruits and salads.

Dig pit 6 inches smaller than grate and 16 inches deep. Line completely with heavy duty aluminum foil. Place 8-inch cinder blocks around edge of pit to support grid and provide room for heat circulation and stoking fire. The distance from pig to coals is 24 inches.

Form two drip pans the length of pit, page 19. Make hood by bending four 6-ft. steel reinforcing rods and attaching to two parallel rods with 16-gauge wire. Cover with heavy duty aluminum foil.

Start fire 2 hours before placing pig on grid. Coals should be ashy grey and glowing to start cooking. Cook a 100-pound pig 6 to 7 hours to an internal temperature of 170°F.

Place pig on grid, skin side up. Place meat thermometer in each ham and shoulder. Prick skin 1 hour into cooking time to minimize flare-ups. Use water gun and pitcher for emergency flare-ups.

Cover pig with hood to create an oven with even heat distribution. Keep the fire low and steady. Stoke the fire by starting coals in a portable grill and adding with shovel. Use 80 to 100 pounds of charcoal throughout the day.

Cook meat to an internal temperature of 150°F before turning. To turn, remove thermometers. Run cookie sheets or large heavy spatulas under pig to loosen. Flip the pig and reinsert thermometers. Re-cover and finish cooking.

Prepare 1½ gallons of Hot and Spicy Sauce, page 34. Baste pig with one-third of sauce after flipping. Serve remaining sauce with pork. Meat is done when internal temperature is 170°F.

How to Barbecue for Two

Make Reynolds Wrap® baking pan large enough for fish fillet pinwheels, page 19. Lightly grease pans.

Sprinkle fillets on all sides with seasoned salt. Place slice of Swiss cheese and a single layer of tomatoes on top of each fillet. Sprinkle with basil leaves.

Roll up each fillet starting at wide end. Place seam side down in aluminum foil pans.

Barbecuing for Two

When barbecuing for two, first consider the amount of food to be cooked on the grill. Less food calls for a smaller grill. Take advantage of small portable covered cookers or portable grills that can be covered with a Reynolds Wrap® hood. Both are easy to clean and store. One saving plus of a smaller grill is that fewer briquets are needed to cook the food.

Plan a menu that requires a minimum of preparation. Individual portion foods like chops, steak or fish fillets are simplest to prepare and serve. Grill the rest of the meal right alongside the main dish.

For an elegant barbecue for two, try fish fillets rolled into pinwheels that are stuffed with fresh tomato, Swiss cheese and basil leaves. Cook with mushrooms and parsley in Reynolds Wrap baking pans. Cover with grill hood or use an aluminum foil hood, page 18. Cook on the grill for a smoky flavor.

To complement the fish, try a vegetable kabob, page 82. Brush thick slices of zucchini, parboiled onions and carrots with a home-made or bottled salad dressing. Include refrigerator rolls with this light elegant meal, page 88. Serve fruit kabobs for dessert, page 90. With proper planning, all can be done on the grill.

Top fish fillets with melted butter, sliced mushrooms and chopped parsley. Arrange, using slow, indirect heat, page 21. Place fillets over coals and biscuits on grill without any coals under biscuit pan.

Cook fillets in covered grill about 18 to 20 minutes or until fish flakes. Heat refrigerator rolls 15 to 20 minutes using medium-low, indirect heat.

Accompany with vegetable skewers of zucchini, parboiled onions and carrots, page 82. Try fruit kabobs for dessert, page 75.

How to Barbecue on a Budget

Place one 4- to 5-pound bone-less beef chuck pot roast in Beer Marinade, page 33. Cover and refrigerate 4 hours or overnight.

Before placing roast on grill, Drugstore Wrap potatoes for grilling, page 81, stuff tomatoes with green pea filling, page 85, and prepare apples for baking, page 90.

Remove roast from marinade, insert meat thermometer, and grill over low, indirect heat 1½ to 2 hours in a covered cooker. Meat is done when the internal temperature reaches 140°F for rare, 160°F for medium.

Barbecue on a Budget

Keep barbecuing costs down by watching for sales on pork, beef, poultry and lamb. The slow roast of the coals adds a smoky flavor to inexpensive roasts that makes them ideal for entertaining. Not only do they serve large groups of people, but roasts in a covered cooker or on a rotisserie require a minimal amount of attention and preparation. For something different on the grill try barbecuing a pot roast. Marinate a beef chuck pot roast in Beer Marinade, page 33, 4 hours or overnight. Then remove from the marinade and cook over low, indirect heat in a covered grill. Serve with tomatoes stuffed with green peas, page 85, foil-baked potatoes, page 83, and all-American baked apples, page 90.

Other economical main dishes include grilled turkey or whole chicken brushed with herb butter or a favorite sauce, pages 34 and 35; whole roasts such as pork butt, page 47; or beef round tip roast, page 41; or stuffed vegetables that can serve as a substitute for meat. Serve bulgur-stuffed green peppers, spinach-stuffed yellow squash or rice-stuffed eggplant, page 84.

Look to in-season produce to round-out the meal. Steam favorite combinations of fresh vegetables in an aluminum foil packet or skewer-cook chunks of vegetables and serve straight from the grill, page 83. When preparing the fire, use only the amount of coals that you need. It is not necessary to overload the grill with too many briquets for an evenly heated fire. For most foods, coals should extend about 1 inch around edge of food, page 21. Use vents on the grill cover and base to snuff out the coals when cooking is done. Coals can be left to cool in grill, then used with fresh briquets at the next cookout.

One hour before meat is done, add foil-wrapped potatoes to grid. Add stuffed tomatoes 30 minutes before meat is done.

Keep an even fire by adding fresh charcoal to the fire every hour. Add a few extra briquets to the coals just before placing the apples on the grill to bake.

Grill apples for 20 minutes over medium coals. Serve with vanilla ice cream, if desired.

Brunch

For a hearty brunch, prepare sausage-biscuit pinwheels and baked eggs. Sausage-biscuits can be prepared by layering refrigerated biscuit dough with a cheesy sausage and apple filling. (See directions below.)

Baked eggs can be cooked alongside sausage-biscuit pinwheels. Butter six Redi-Pan® Muffin Cups. Place over medium-low coals in covered grill. Place one egg in each cup; season with salt and pepper. Bake in covered grill for 12 to 15 minutes or until desired doneness.

For a lighter menu, use a Redi-Pan Mini-Casserole Pan to fry eggs, page 51. Grill sausages along with eggs, directly on grid or steamed in an aluminum foil packet, page 51. Cook muffins in a covered grill, page 88, or toast English muffins, cut side down, several minutes over hot coals. If grill is large enough, heat coffee over low coals toward back of grill.

How to Grill a Brunch

Place one can (11 oz.) of 10 refrigerated biscuits on floured surface; flatten with hands and pinch seams together. Roll out to form a 12 × 8-inch rectangle.

Sprinkle evenly with ¾ pound cooked and crumbled pork sausage, 2 tablespoons chopped onion, 1 cup grated Colby cheese, ½ cup chopped apple, 1 tablespoon brown sugar and ¼ teaspoon ground cinnamon.

Roll up dough starting at short side. Cut roll into six slices. Place in two greased Redi-Pan Round Cake Pans. Bake in covered grill over medium-low, indirect coals 30 to 35 minutes.

Tailgating

Tailgate barbecues start with a sturdy portable grill, the basic barbecue utensils to aid handling, a box of Heavy Duty Reynolds Wrap® to simplify cooking and cleanup, and the briquets. Select instant lighting briquets that do not require charcoal starter for easiest, most reliable fire.

Use Reynolds Wrap aluminum foil to mold saucepots that will hold hearty soups and chili instead of bringing heavy pots. See page 19. Plan a menu substantial enough to satisfy big appetites. Try the hearty chili and sausage sandwich menu. You can top with your favorite cookies wrapped in individual bundles or a prebaked cake.

For easy transporation be sure to line grill with heavy duty aluminum foil so ashes can be easily wrapped and disposed of when cooled. Wrap the soiled grid in aluminum foil before returning it to the car.

How to Have a Tailgate Barbecue

Hearty Sausage Sandwiches. Split smoked sausage links. Grill over medium-hot, direct coals 5 minutes or until heated through. Turn often; serve in French bread rolls topped with individual servings of Vegetable Trio.

Vegetable Trio. Prepare at home a Bundle Wrap of ¼ cup chopped green pepper, ¼ cup chopped onion, ½ cup sliced fresh mushrooms and 1 tablespoon butter for each person. At tailgate, grill over medium-hot coals 10 minutes.

Hearty Chili. Heat your favorite chili over medium-hot coals in a Reynolds Wrap saucepan, page 19. For a shortcut, warm canned chili and top with shredded Cheddar cheese.

Texas Rib Party

Plan a Texas rib party when you want to feed an extra large group. This is the time to make use of a large covered grill and plenty of wire rib racks. Use a long-handled brush to baste ribs while cooking. Steam ribs in aluminum foil before placing on grill to avoid flare-ups, page 48. Serve the ribs with grilled nachos, page 93, corn-on-the-grill, page 81, Texas toast, cole-slaw and cherry pie, page 31.

Nachos. Start with several Redi-Pan® Toaster Oven Trays filled with nacho appetizers. Cover the pans with a single layer of tortilla chips. Top each chip with Monterey Jack cheese and jalapeño peppers, page 93.

Ribs. Prepare Hot and Spicy Barbecue Sauce, page 34, for basting. Begin cooking ribs in an aluminum foil packet to render fat and finish cooking directly on grid, page 49.

Corn and Coleslaw. Grill foil-wrapped corn or Bundle Wrapped corn, pepper and onions, page 83, directly over coals. Accompany with your favorite coleslaw.

Texas Toast. Cut French bread into ¾-inch slices. Brush with Garlic Butter, page 35. Toast on both sides over direct coals.

Cherry Pie. Buy a bakery cherry pie or bake your own in a disposable aluminum foilware pie pan. Overwrap by using Bundle Wrap and heat in a covered cooker, page 31.

Clambake

Even if you don't live at the beach, you can enjoy an impressive backyard clambake. Simply substitute a combination of greens and damp cheesecloth for seaweed, firewood for driftwood and heavy duty aluminum foil for the traditional sand covering. About 12 pounds of mixed greens (collard greens, kale, etc.) and 15 yards of cheesecloth will hold in moisture as the food cooks. Three rolls of 37½-ft. heavy duty aluminum foil will both line and seal pit. Use about 100 pounds of completely dry rocks (size of grapefruit) to line pit and hold in heat as food cooks.

For a party of eight, plan on layering eight baking or sweet potatoes, eight ears of corn, eight onions, eight chicken halves, eight live lobsters and 4 to 8 dozen clams. Prepare your favorite clam chowder as an appetizer. Serve clambake with plenty of melted butter, lemons and watermelon.

How to Clambake

Dig a bowl-shaped pit 3 ft. in diameter and 1½ ft. deep in the center. Using crisscross pattern, line with double thickness of heavy duty aluminum foil, then a layer of dry rocks about the size of grapefruit. NOTE: Wet rocks can explode.

Build a bonfire on top of rocks in the pit. Use firewood and kindling. Let the fire burn 1½ to 2 hours or until burned down and rocks are hot. NOTE: Do not use charcoal.

Soak corn-on-the-cob (with silk removed) and mixed greens in cold water while fire is burning. Wash clams and set aside. Peel onions; remove ends. Oil potatoes. Refrigerate lobster on ice.

Once fire has burned down, work quickly to prevent rocks from losing heat. Tamp down embers. On top of rocks, layer pit in the following order: half the greens, strips of wet cheesecloth, potatoes, corn, onions, chicken halves, live lobsters and clams.

Cover food with remaining wet cheesecloth, then greens. Cover pit with heavy duty aluminum foil. Crimp all sides to the edges of the aluminum foil used to line the pit. Let food steam-cook 40 to 60 minutes.

Remove foods immediately when done. Cooking times will vary depending on temperature of rocks. Peek at clams after 40 minutes. If they are open and lobsters are bright red, dinner is ready. Serve with melted butter and lemon.

Index

A

Accessories, 14
Accessories You Can Make, 18
Begin With the Basics, 16
How to Make an Aluminum Foil
  Hood, 18
How to Make an Aluminum Foil
  Wind Shield, 18
Appetizers & Snacks, 92
Barbecued Party Wings, 93
How to Grill Appetizers and
  Snacks, 93
Nachos, 93
Oysters and Clams, 93
Popcorn, 93
Smoked Fish Log, 93
Apples,
Apple Curry Sauce, 34
Apple Tarragon Marinade, 33
Baked Apple, 90
Curry Apple Marinade, 33
Apricot Ginger Sauce, 34

B

Baked Apple, 90
Baked Fish with Herbs and
  Lemon, 67
Baked Fish with Vegetables, 67
Barbecue Basics, 7
Barbecue on a Budget, 103
Barbecue Sauce,
  Lamb Sauces and Seasonings
    Chart, 53
  Sauce Chart, 34
Barbecued Party Wings, 93
Barbecuing for Two, 101
Barbecuing the Perfect Burger, 38
Beans, 83
Beef, 36
Barbecuing the Perfect Burger, 38
Beef Roast Chart, 41
Beef Roasts, 41
Hamburger Variations, 38
How to Barbecue Burgers, 39
How to Barbecue Roasts, 41
How to Barbecue Steaks, 40
Kabob Chart, 74
Rib Chart, 49
Steak, 40
Biscuits,
  How to Barbecue Refrigerator
    Biscuits and Rolls, 88
Blue Cheese Butter, 35

Brazier,
  see Grills
Breads,
Breads & Desserts, 86
Grilled Open-Faced Sandwich, 89
Ham and Cheese Loaf, 89
How to Bake Frozen Bread
  Loaf, 89
How to Barbecue Refrigerator
  Biscuits and Rolls, 88
How to Grill Pre-Baked Bread, 87
How to Make Cornbread on the
  Grill, 89
Muffins in a Covered Grill, 88
Pocket Bread Sandwiches, 89
Stuffed Stromboli, 89
Brisket,
  Fresh Beef Brisket, 41
Brunch, 104
Budget,
  Barbecue on a Budget, 103
Bundle-Wrapped Chicken
  Dinner, 61
Bundle Wrap, How to, 29
Burgers,
Barbecuing the Perfect Burger, 38
Hamburger Variations, 38
How to Barbecue Burgers, 39
Pork Burger Chart, 43
Pork Chops, Steaks and Burgers
  Chart, 45
Butters, 35
Butter Chart, 35
How to Use Butters, 35
Marinades, Sauces & Butters, 32

C

Cakes,
  Gingerbread, 91
Carrots, 83
Cheese,
Blue Cheese Butter, 35
Cheese Herb Butter, 35
Ham and Cheese Loaf, 89
Smoked Fish Log, 93
Chicken,
Barbecued Party Wings, 93
Bundle-Wrapped Chicken
  Dinner, 61
How to Barbecue Chicken, 57
How to Bundle Wrap a Chicken
  Dinner, 58
How to Grill Chicken in a
  Basket, 58
Poultry Chart, 60
Poultry Variations Chart, 61
Clams,
Clambake, 108
Clams and Oysters, 69

How to Clambake, 108
How to Smoke Oysters and
  Clams, 70
Oysters and Clams, 93
Complete Grill Meals, 96
Barbecue on a Budget, 103
Barbecuing for Two, 101
Brunch, 104
Clambake, 108
Pig Roast, 99
Tailgating, 105
Texas Rib Party, 106
Cookies,
  Peanut Butter Cookies, 91
Corn, 83
Cornbread,
  How to Make Cornbread on the
    Grill, 89
Cornish Hens,
  Poultry Chart, 60
  Poultry Variations Chart, 61
Covered Cooker, 11
  Covered Cooker Method,
    Ribs, 48
  Three Ways to Use Your
    Covered Cooker, 11
Covered Cooking, 25
  Roasting on the Covered Grill, 47
Crab,
  Lobster and Crab, 69
Crown Roasts,
  Rib Crown Roast, 47
Cucumber Sauce, 34

D

Desserts,
Baked Apple, 90
Breads & Desserts, 86
Gingerbread, 91
Lemon Sauce, 91
Peanut Butter Cookies, 91
Pie, 90
Pineapple Kabobs, 90
Drugstore Wrap, How to, 29
Duck,
Domestic Duck, 60
Grilled Duckling, 61
How to Barbecue Duck and
  Game Hens, 57
How to Barbecue Whole Wild
  Duck, 78
Poultry Chart, 60
Poultry Variations Chart, 61

E

Eggplant,
  How to Stuff Eggplant, 84

Vegetable Chart, 83
Ember Cooking, 28
  How to Ember Cook an
    Onion, 28
  How to Ember Cook
    Vegetables, 28

F

Family Barbecue, 96
Fire, 21
Fish,
  Baked Fish with Herbs and
    Lemon, 67
  Baked Fish with Vegetables, 67
  Fish & Seafood, 62
  Fish and Seafood Kabob, 75
  Fish Recipe Chart, 67
  Grilling Time for Fish, 64
  How to Bake Fish in Aluminum
    Foil Packets, 65
  How to Grill Fish Directly
    on Grid, 67
  How to Grill Fish in Flat Spit
    Basket, 66
  How to Grill Fish in Hinged Grill
    Basket, 66
  How to Know if Fish is Done, 64
  How to Make Reynolds Wrap
    Loops, 67
  How to Poach Fish in Individual
    Aluminum Foil Packets, 65
  How to Smoke Fish in a
    Covered Grill, 71
  How to Smoke Fish in a Water
    Smoker, 71
  How to Stuff and Cook Whole
    Fish, 65
  Shellfish, 68
  Smoked Fish Log, 93
  Smoking Fish and Shellfish, 70
  Stuffing for Whole Fish, 67
Fruits,
  Also see individual fruits
  Fruit Kabob, 75

G

Game, 76
  How to Barbecue Pheasant, 78
  How to Barbecue Quail, 77
  How to Barbecue Rabbit, 77
  How to Barbecue Whole Wild
    Duck, 78
  How to Grill Whole Goose, 78
  How to Prepare Venison
    Roast, 79
  How to Prepare Venison
    Steaks, 79

Game Hens,
  How to Barbecue Duck and
    Game Hens, 57
Garlic Butter, 35
Gas Grill, 13
Gingerbread, 91
Glossary of Terms, 7
Goose,
  How to Grill Whole Goose, 78
Grills, 8
  Portable, Tabletop Grills, 13
  Roasting on the Covered Grill, 47
  Selecting a Grill, 9
  The Covered Cooker, 11
  The Gas Grill, 13
  The Open Brazier, 10
  The Water Smoker, 12
Ground Beef,
  see Hamburgers

H

Ham,
  see Pork
Hamburgers,
  Barbecuing the Perfect
    Burger, 38
  Ground Beef Kabobs, 75
  Hamburger Variations Chart, 38
  How to Barbecue Burgers, 39

I

Italian Baste, 53

K

Kabobs, 72
  How to Prepare Food for
    Skewers, 73
  Kabob Chart, 74
  Kabobs from Leg, Lamb
    Chart, 53
  Pineapple Kabobs, 90
  Pork Kabobs, 45
  Poultry Kabobs with Stir-Fried
    Vegetables, 61
  Tips for Kabob-ing, 74

L

Lamb, 52
  How to Cook Different Cuts of
    Lamb, 52
  Lamb Chart, 53
  Lamb Kabob, 75
  Lamb Sauces and Seasonings
    Chart, 53
Lemon Sauce, 91

Lobster,
  Lobster and Crab, 69
  Rock Lobster Tails, 69

M

Marinades,
  How to Marinate, 33
  Marinade Chart, 33
  Marinades, Sauces & Butters, 32
Meats,
  see individual meats
Menus, 94
Mint Honey Marinade, 33
Muffins in a Covered Grill, 88
Mushrooms, 83
Mussels, 68
Mustard Butter, 35
Mustard Dill Sauce, 53

N

Nachos, 93

O

Onions,
  How to Ember Cook an
    Onion, 28
  Onion Soup Marinade, 33
  Vegetable Chart, 83
Open Brazier, 10
  Open Brazier Method, 24
  Open Brazier Method, Ribs, 48
  Three Ways to Use Your
    Brazier, 10
Oysters,
  Clams and Oysters, 69
  How to Smoke Oysters and
    Clams, 70
  Oysters and Clams, 93

P

Parsley Orange Butter, 35
Peanut Butter Cookies, 91
Peppers, 83
Pheasant, 78
Pie, 90
Pig Roast, 99
Pineapple,
  Pineapple Chutney Sauce, 53
  Pineapple Kabobs, 90
  Pineapple Marinade, 33
  Pineapple Sauce, 34
Pocket Bread Sandwiches, 89
Popcorn, 93
Pork, 42
  Baby Back Ribs, 49

Country-Style Ribs, 49
General Tips on Grilling Pork, 45
Ground Pork Burgers, 45
Ground Pork Kabob, 75
Ham and Cheese Loaf, 89
How to Prepare Ground Pork
  for Barbecuing, 43
How to Prepare Pork Chops, 44
Pig Roast, 99
Pork Burger Chart, 43
Pork Chops, Steaks and Burgers
  Chart, 45
Pork Roast Chart, 47
Pork Roasts, 46
Rib Chart, 49
Ribs, 48
Spareribs, 49
Two Methods for Grilling Pork
  Roasts, 47
Potatoes, 83
Poultry, 54
  Also see Chicken, Duck, Game
  Hens and Turkey

Q

Quail,
  How to Barbecue Quail, 77

R

Rabbit,
  How to Barbecue Rabbit, 77
Red Wine Marinade, 33
Ribs, 48
  Baby Back Ribs, 49
  Beef Ribs, 49
  Country-Style Ribs, 49
  How to Steam Ribs, 48
  Rib Chart, 49
  Spareribs, 49
  Three Ways to Grill Ribs, 49
Rolls, 88
  How to Barbecue Refrigerator
  Biscuits and Rolls, 88
Rotisserie,
  How to Rotisserie Other Types
  of Poultry, 59
  Rotisserie Cooking, 26
  Rotisserie Techniques, 26

S

Sandwiches,
  Grilled Open-Faced
  Sandwich, 89
  Ham and Cheese Loaf, 89
  Pocket Bread Sandwiches, 89
  Sandwich Chart, 89

Stuffed Stromboli, 89
Sauces, 34
  Lamb Sauces and Seasonings
  Chart, 53
  Lemon Sauce, 91
  Marinades, Sauces & Butters, 32
  Sauce Chart, 34
Sausages, 50
  Fresh Sausage, 50
  Fully Cooked Sausage, 50
  How to Barbecue Sausages, 51
  Sausage Kabob, 75
  Sausage Types for Grilling, 50
Seafood,
  See Fish and Shellfish
Shellfish, 68
  Clambake, 108
  Clams and Oysters, 69
  Fish & Seafood, 62
  Fish and Seafood Kabob, 75
  How to Clambake, 108
  How to Smoke Oysters and
  Clams, 70
  Lobster and Crab, 69
  Mussels, 68
  Oysters and Clams, 93
  Rock Lobster Tails, 69
  Shrimp, 68
  Smoking Fish and Shellfish, 70
Shrimp, 68
Smoke Cooking, 27
Smoked Fish Log, 93
Smoked Ham Half, 47
Smoked Loin Chops, Pork, 45
Smoker,
  How to Smoke Fish in a Water
  Smoker, 71
  The Water Smoker, 12
  Two Ways to Use Your Water
  Smoker, 12
Smoking Fish and Shellfish, 70
Snacks,
  see Appetizers & Snacks, 92
Spareribs, 49
Squash,
  Summer Squash, 83
  Winter Squash, 83
Stir Fry,
  How to Stir Fry Over the
  Coals, 82
  Poultry Kabobs with Stir-Fried
  Vegetables, 61
Stromboli,
  Stuffed Stromboli, 89
Stuffed Vegetable Meals, 84
Stuffing,
  How to Cook Stuffing While
  Grilling Poultry, 60
  Stuffing for Whole Fish, 67

T

Tailgating, 105
Tangy Beer Sauce, 34
Teriyaki Marinade, 33
Texas Rib Party, 106
Time Plan, Making a, 95
Tomatoes, 83
Turkey,
  How to Barbecue Turkey, 57
  Poultry Chart, 60
  Poultry Variations Chart, 61
  Turkey Breast with Vegetable
  Casserole, 61

U

Utensils,
  see Accessories

V

Vegetables, 80
  Also see individual vegetables
  Baked Fish with Vegetables, 67
  How to Ember Cook, 81
  How to Ember Cook
  Vegetables, 28
  How to Foil Wrap, 81
  How to Grill Directly on Grid, 82
  How to Skewer Cook
  Vegetables, 82
  How to Stir Fry Over the
  Coals, 82
  How to Stuff Vegetables, 85
  Poultry Kabobs with Stir-Fried
  Vegetables, 61
  Stuffed Vegetable Meals, 84
  Turkey Breast with Vegetable
  Casserole, 61
  Vegetable Chart, 83
  Vegetable Kabob, 75
Venison,
  How to Prepare Venison
  Roast, 79
  How to Prepare Venison
  Steaks, 79

W

Wine,
  Red Wine Marinade, 33
  White Wine Marinade, 33
Wrapping Techniques, 29
  How to Bundle Wrap, 29
  How to Bundle Wrap a Chicken
  Dinner, 58
  How to Drugstore Wrap, 29